"ADD in adults is turning out to be among the most impairing disorders seen in outpatient mental health clinics in terms of the number of major life activities that it adversely affects and the severity with which it impacts each of them. One such domain is that of money management. In this first-ever book devoted to the impact of adult ADD on one's financial life, the authors do a masterful job of both providing a review of the most common problem areas adults with ADD are likely to experience as well as a richly detailed set of recommendations for how best to try and resolve those problems. The book will be of tremendous benefit to not only adults with ADD, but their spouses/partners, parents or other family members, and clinicians who routinely specialize in the diagnosis and treatment of ADD in adults."

—Russell A. Barkley, Ph.D., clinical professor of psychiatry at Medical University of South Carolina and research professor of psychiatry at SUNY Upstate Medical University

"The guidelines and inventories in this self-help manual can enable people with ADD to make the most of their treatment. While medicine improves core symptom problems, these financial management skills can further reduce ADD consequences and impairments."

—Richard L. Rubin, MD, director of Vermont Clinical Study Center and adjunct associate professor at Dartmouth Medical College

D1596343

"*ADD and Your Money* is a long-needed and critical resource for adults with ADD. It is reader-friendly, accessible, and full of wonderful strategies. This book is guaranteed to help anyone who struggles with finances as well as individuals who want to learn money management skills or who simply desire to become more fiscally responsible. Thank you for this valuable contribution!"

—Nancy A. Ratey, Ed.M., MCC, SCAC, strategic life coach and author of *The Disorganized Mind*

"If you have ADD, your financial future may depend on reading this book. You'll be amazed to see such practical, easy-to-follow advice for your biggest financial headaches."

—Lara Honos-Webb, Ph.D., author of *The Gift of ADHD* and *Listening to Depression*

ADD
AND YOUR
MONEY

A Guide to
Personal Finance for Adults with
Attention **D**eficit **D**isorder

Stephanie Moulton Sarkis, Ph.D.
Karl Klein, JD

New Harbinger Publications, Inc.

Publisher's Note

The material in this book is published solely for general informational purposes and does not take into account the specific investment objectives, financial situation, or particular needs of any reader. It is provided with the understanding that neither the authors nor the publisher is engaged in rendering financial, legal, accounting, tax or other professional advice or services by providing this book. You should assess whether the information is appropriate for you and talk with a licensed, qualified financial or other professional adviser before making an investment or financial decision. The contents of this book are not to be relied upon as a substitute for such financial or other professional advice.

The opinions contained herein and references made to third parties are based on information obtained from sources believed to be reliable, but are not guaranteed as being accurate. Readers should not regard it as a substitute for the exercise of their own judgment.

The publisher and authors accept no liability whatsoever for any loss or damage of any kind arising out of the use of all or any part of this material, including but not limited to loss of profit or any other commercial damages, incidental, consequential, special or other damages.

Distributed in Canada by Raincoast Books

Copyright © 2009 by Stephanie Moulton Sarkis and Karl Klein
New Harbinger Publications, Inc.
5674 Shattuck Avenue
Oakland, CA 94609
www.newharbinger.com

FSC
Mixed Sources
Product group from well-managed
forests and other controlled sources

Cert no. SW-COC-002283
www.fsc.org
© 1996 Forest Stewardship Council

All Rights Reserved
Printed in the United States of America

Acquired by Melisaa Kirk; Cover design by Amy Shoup;
Edited by Elisabeth Beller; Text design by Tracy Marie Carlson

Library of Congress Cataloging-in-Publication Data

Sarkis, Stephanie.
  ADD and your money : a guide to personal finance for adults with attention deficit disorder / Stephanie Moulton Sarkis and Karl Klein ; foreword by Harvey C. Parker.
    p. cm.
  Includes bibliographical references.
  ISBN-13: 978-1-57224-707-9 (pbk. : alk. paper)
  ISBN-10: 1-57224-707-X (pbk. : alk. paper) 1. Attention-deficit disorder in adults--Popular works. 2. Finance, Personal. 3. People with mental disabilities--Finance, Personal. 4. People with mental disabilities--Life skills guides. I. Klein, Karl, JD. II. Title.
  RC394.A85S263 2009
  332.0240087'5--dc22

                          2009038439

11 10 09   10 9 8 7 6 5 4 3 2 1   First printing

Contents

Foreword

During the past twenty-five years, a small but growing body of scientific literature has been published on the nature of attention-deficit/hyperactivity disorder (ADHD) in the adult population. ADHD was once thought to be the exclusive domain of children and adolescents, but scientists and practitioners have found that ADHD symptoms found in youth often cross into adulthood and have profound effects on many aspects of adult living.

Much of what has been written about adults with ADHD has come from the experience of clinicians who treat adults with this condition and from the adults themselves. The growing body of this anecdotal literature strongly concludes that adults with ADHD are frequently severely impacted by the nature of their condition. Furthermore, there is a growing body of scientific literature (Barkley, Murphy, and Fischer 2008) that supports this conclusion as well. Among the myriad problems that are reported by adults with ADHD are underachievement in school and on the job, relationship difficulties, problems with organization, problems with attention regulation, self-control difficulties, anxiety and depression, and financial problems.

Indeed, scientific studies of adults with ADHD found money management to be a significant problem. Adults with ADHD had greater problems than their non-ADHD counterparts in several areas of money management:

- Managing money
- Saving money
- Buying on impulse
- Nonpayment for utilities

- Missing loan payments

- Exceeding credit card limits

- Having a poor credit rating

- Not saving for retirement

Why are money management problems so prevalent in adults with ADHD? These problems may stem, in part, from *executive function deficits* that are at the core of ADHD and that explain symptom development. Such deficits make it difficult to plan, organize, and inhibit behavior—skills that are important for good money management in addition to many other aspects of daily life.

People with ADHD are often "managed" by the moment and sometimes have greater difficulty taking a long view of things. Planning a budget for both the short term and the long term, organizing bills so they are paid on time, delaying purchases, resisting impulsive spending, and saving for the future might come naturally or easily to many people, but these actions require much greater effort and focus from those with ADHD.

What I like about this book is how the authors' ideas and advice is tailored specifically to those with ADHD and gets at the heart of their issues. For example, the authors recognize the difficulty that adults with ADHD have when it comes to detailed, monotonous work such as the bill paying and financial record keeping that is essential to good money management. With this in mind, the authors review several ADHD-friendly strategies to manage these tasks: use of money management software and online banking, novel ways to organize, and alternative payment methods that can simplify the often tedious bill-paying process, organization of receipts, and so on.

The authors also point out the importance of having a budget for good money management. Just as a successful business follows a business plan that outlines the company's goals, so would most people benefit from having a plan to accomplish their immediate, midterm, and long-term financial goals. A budget is frequently an important part of such a plan, because it can help you see clearly what your routine or fixed expenses are, how much money you need for basic necessities (your needs), what may be left over for optional purchases (your wants), and what extra you might have left for emergencies and for savings.

Of course, everyone has times when they've made an impulsive purchase—one that they didn't plan for or think through ahead of time. Most budgets can handle a little of this, but when spending gets out of control, budgets get wiped out and goals can be very hard to accomplish. Impulsivity is the hallmark of many adults with ADHD, and budgets often crash due to impulse buying. This book is chock-full of helpful ideas to plan a budget and curb impulsive spending: shop with a friend who can help you set limits, look but don't touch items on store shelves, make a shopping list ahead of time and stick to it, spend only the cash you have, and so on.

Good money management, however, is certainly not only about self-discipline. Success requires that you and your partner also have similar financial goals, that you spend wisely, understand different investment products for saving and building your assets, consider the best options when you need to borrow money, identify methods for pension planning, and so on.

I know that by reading this book you will be enriched by the practical advice that it contains for anyone who wants to learn more about money management. However, it will be particularly invaluable for adults with ADHD who want to break bad habits and replace them with new skills that will lead to a healthier financial future.

—Harvey C. Parker, Ph.D.
    Cofounder, Children and Adults with
    Attention-Deficit/Hyperactivity Disorder, and author

Introduction

If you have Attention deficit disorder (ADD), you know that it can affect your ability to keep track of your finances and save up money for your future. You may have struggled with debt or impulsive spending. Maybe you have had a relationship fall apart because your partner thought you were irresponsible with money. All of these problems are difficult and painful, not to mention inconvenient and expensive. They are also more common when you have ADD.

This book can help. Stephanie is an ADD coach and the author of two successful books about living with ADD. Karl is a corporate attorney and has an educational background in finance. Together they will show you how to resolve conflicts about money with your spouse; weather life changes like marriage, divorce, births, death, and medical catastrophes; invest your money wisely; organize your finances in a way that is easy to maintain; budget wisely; spend responsibly; manage loans and debts; make the best use of bank services; and teach your children about money.

With some perseverance and the tools in this book, you can overcome the financial challenges you have faced due to your distraction and impulsivity. There is hope for you to have a successful future and a good relationship with money.

WHAT IS ADD?

Attention deficit disorder (ADD) is a genetic disorder that affects 4.4 percent of the U.S. population (Kessler et al. 2006). If you have ADD, there is a 75 percent chance that you inherited ADD genes from at least one of your parents (Rietveld et al. 2004).

The Use of "ADD" vs. "ADHD"

You probably have heard both the terms "ADD" and "ADHD" used to describe a pattern of inattention and impulsivity. While the proper clinical term is "ADHD" (even if you do not have hyperactivity), the most common term used by the public is "ADD." Therefore, in the remainder of the book, we will use the term "ADD."

Types of ADD

There are three subtypes of ADD: inattentive, hyperactive/impulsive, and combined (American Psychiatric Association 2004).

Symptoms of the Inattentive Subtype

- Distractibility

- Disorganization

- Difficulty paying attention to detail

- Forgetfulness

- Difficulty focusing during tasks

- Difficulty following through with tasks

- Avoiding tasks that require sustained mental effort

- Losing items often

- Not appearing to listen when spoken to

To meet criteria for the inattentive type of ADD, at least six out of nine inattention symptoms must be met.

Symptoms of the Hyperactive/Impulsive Subtype

■ Often "on the go" or acts as if "driven by a motor"

■ Fidgetiness

■ Excessive running or climbing, or a feeling of inner restlessness

■ Excessive talking

■ Difficulty engaging in leisure activities quietly

■ Interrupting or intruding on others

■ Leaving seat when remaining seated is expected

■ Blurting out answers before questions are completed

■ Difficulty waiting turns or standing in line

To meet the criteria for this subtype, you must have at least six out of nine hyperactive/impulsive symptoms. If you have six out of nine symptoms for both the inattentive and hyperactive/impulsive subtypes, you may have the combined subtype of ADD.

In addition, according to diagnostic criteria, ADD symptoms must have been present since the age of seven. About 50 percent of people retain symptoms of ADD into adulthood (Wilens 2004). However, as an adult, you may experience your symptoms a little differently than you did in childhood. An adult with ADD can appear less hyperactive than a child with ADD. For example, instead of climbing on the furniture, you may now have a feeling of inner restlessness.

ADD and the Brain

People with ADD have difficulties with *executive functions,* which are processes located in the brain's frontal lobes. Executive functions include tasks such as processing information, initiating tasks, regulating moods, planning future behavior, and learning from consequences (Barkley 2005). In a study by Biederman et al. (2006), adults with ADD had significantly more deficits of executive functioning than those without ADD. In addition, the adults with ADD had a significantly lower socioeconomic status, lower academic achievement, and significant functional impairment compared to those without ADD.

HOW ADD AFFECTS MONEY MANAGEMENT

Not only does ADD affect scholastic performance, work performance, and the quality of your relationships, it also affects your ability to earn, keep, and manage money. Studies have shown that people with ADD have a greater amount of debt, more difficulty paying their bills, and less money saved up than people without ADD. People with ADD have lower incomes than those without ADD, even when they have a similar education level (Barkley, Murphy, and Fischer 2008). People with ADD also miss more days of work due to "unofficial" absences (Secnik, Swensen, and Lage 2005). They are also more likely to take risks that lead to a loss of money (Dreschler, Rizzo, and Steinhausen 2008).

In addition, people with ADD have higher medical costs, prescription drug costs (for all medications, not just those for ADD), and more total medical costs than those without ADD (Secnik, Swensen, and Lage 2005).

There are several books available regarding money management. However, these books can be overwhelming—they can be too detailed and are not written specifically for a person with ADD. And while those books may give you the tools for getting started on your plan to regain control of your money, it can be difficult to keep up the money management and organization tips that these books offer. For people with ADD, maintaining a new behavior, such as learning to use money management software, can be more difficult than getting that new behavior started.

Financial Portrait of a Person with ADD

If you have ADD, you may have found yourself experiencing one or more of the following:

- You lose time and money due to your inability to stay organized.

- You bounce checks.

- You pay your taxes late or wait until the last minute. You may even be in trouble with the IRS.

- You have lost money on tax deductions because you don't keep track of your receipts.

- You get late fees on your bills because you forget to pay them on time.

- You make impulsive purchases.

- You pay extra to get out of what you consider to be detailed and boring tasks, such as washing your car or mowing the lawn.

- You buy items at the last minute, resulting in a higher cost to you.

- You don't know where to find important financial documents.

- You have a poor credit rating due to late payments or defaulting on loans.

- You "guestimate" how much money you have in your accounts.

- You have a significant amount of credit card debt, and you may even have difficulty making the minimum payments.

- You have considered filing for bankruptcy due to poor money management.

- You have never balanced your checkbook. You may not even be sure what that means.

- You frequently argue with your spouse/partner about your lack of money management skills.

Even if you are currently experiencing several of these issues, there is still hope for you. Continue reading to find out what your life will look like when you become comfortable with money management.

Financial Portrait of a Person with Good Money Management Skills

You have just read (or experienced firsthand) what the combination of ADD and poor money management looks like. For a contrast, here's how to recognize someone with good money management skills. When you want to improve your money management skills, it's important to have a positive idea of what a person with good financial sense looks like:

- Understands the value of money but does not let it control his life

- Lives beneath her means—doesn't spend more than she earns

- Has an emergency savings fund equal to three or more months of living expenses

- Has a good credit history

- Educates his children about saving and spending

- Has a limited amount of debt or no debt

- Understands that minor financial setbacks can be normal and are fixable

- Educates herself about money management by reading books, websites, and/or the newspaper

- Plans ahead before going to the store to avoid buying items at the last minute

- Can locate financial documents fairly quickly and has those papers filed in a systemized manner

- Stays away from extended warranties

- Looks for the best deal on an item (within reason)

- Has a list of immediate and long-term financial goals

- Uses money management software and updates it regularly

These may seem like unobtainable or unrealistic goals to you right now, but you do have the ability to be successful at money management. Continue reading to learn how to reach your potential.

The Link Between ADD Medication and Financial Success

If you have been diagnosed with ADD, you may want to consider taking medication to reduce your symptoms. One of the benefits of medication is that you become better organized and better able to prioritize—which can make you better able to manage your money. Also, medication can actually help people with ADD accrue more money. In a study by Cynthia Pietras and colleagues (2003), study subjects who were on stimulant medication chose to wait a longer time to receive a larger amount of money rather than wait a short period of time for a smaller amount of money. Those who were not on stimulant medication were significantly more likely to choose the short wait, suggesting that someone with ADD who is not on medication may have difficulty seeing the long-term benefits of saving up money or investing.

You may be concerned that taking medication for ADD may increase your risk for addiction. However, studies show that taking stimulant medication actually decreases your chances of abusing substances (Biederman, Monuteaux et al. 2008). Not only that, but the risk of substance abuse decreases significantly the earlier in life a person starts taking medication (Mannuzza et al. 2008). In addition, there are nonstimulant medications available for the treatment of ADD. Speak with your doctor if you are interested in medication treatment for ADD.

TODAY'S FINANCIAL CLIMATE

In addition to the money management difficulties you may be experiencing, the current economy has made the process even more challenging. In March 2009, bankruptcy filings increased 24 percent in one month and increased 41 percent from the same time period in 2008. It is predicted that there will be 1.4 million bankruptcy filings in 2009 (American Bankruptcy Institute 2009). Many people are feeling anxiety from the financial crunch. For people with ADD, this feeling of panic is magnified, especially when people generally considered financially savvy are now filing for bankruptcy.

MONEY MANAGEMENT SKILLS CAN BE LEARNED

Up to this point in the book, the information you have read may seem pessimistic. However, just by being aware of the relationship between ADD and money management, you are headed in the right direction. Money management can seem scary and daunting at first, but after you jump in, you usually find that you have more money (and hope) than you originally thought. And there is something powerful about being able to know how much money you have in the bank and watching that amount grow due to your newly honed money management skills.

It's important to remember that money has no intrinsic value. It is neither good nor bad; it just is. Money is simply a tool for obtaining the things you need and want in life. When you take away the emotional value you have placed on money, it can be much easier to deal with it. Remember that from this point on, you are starting anew, regardless of the difficulties you have had with money management in the past.

WHY THIS BOOK IS USEFUL

The goal of this book is to help free you from money worries and increase your ability to be financially successful. You may have suffered from insomnia due to anxiety over how you are going to pay this month's bills, save up enough money for retirement, or avoid foreclosure and/or bankruptcy. When you have a good grasp of your money situation, you are able to sleep better at night—money worries no longer wake you from your slumber.

Most people with ADD tend to be competitive, so it helps to view money management as a kind of game: you and your money are on one side of the field, and banks, lenders, and creditors are on the other. This book will help you understand the game so that you can not only learn to "play" it successfully, but can also work cooperatively with the other "team" to further ensure your success.

INSIDE THIS BOOK

In the first chapter, you will learn how your money management challenges affect your relationship with your spouse or partner. Chapter 2 details how life events such as marriage and divorce (which happen at a higher rate in the ADD population than in the general population) affect finances (Barkley, Murphy, and Fischer 2008). People with ADD can have difficulty visualizing long-term needs, so in chapter 3, you will learn about financial planning for your future, including your retirement. Chapter 4 gives details on investing in a way that is understandable and applicable to your life. You will also learn about the different types of financial professionals and how they can best help you. Chapter 5 will help you organize your money in a way that is ADD-friendly, including offering solutions for the zillions of receipts that take up space in your home.

Chapter 6 will show you how to set up a budget that you can follow *and* stick to over time. Chapter 7 will teach you the joys of rational spending, including information on what you definitely don't want to skimp on. Chapter 8 will tell you about the different types of debt and teach you how to get control of the debt in your life. You will learn about bank services, including electronic banking, in chapter 9, and chapter 10 will give you tips on teaching your kids about responsible money management. There is also a Resources section at the end of the book.

Money Terms Used in This Book

You may be familiar with several of the terms in this book, while other terms may leave you scratching your head in confusion. Here's a quick glossary:

- *Asset*—any valuable item, especially something that can be converted into cash

- *Bankruptcy*—a legal process whereby a judge eliminates your debt or creates a payment plan that you must follow

- *Budget*—a realistic list of your expected income and expenses for a certain period of time

- *Debt*—a promise to pay or give something back to another person *Mortgage*—a loan to finance the purchase of real estate (typically with periodic payments and a stated interest rate) along with an agreement to sell some property, usually a house or condo, if you fail to pay the loan back on time

- *Insurance*—an agreement a company makes that, in exchange for a small payment from you, the company agrees to make a much larger payment in case of a loss

- *Investing*—putting money or capital into a business with the expectation of profit

- *Loan*—a promise to pay someone back if they give you money (called a *promissory note* if written on paper)

- *Will*—a legal document that says what should happen to your personal belongings and money after your death

CHAPTER 1

ADD, Money, and Relationships

In any relationship (whether or not one or both partners have ADD), money can be a major source of conflict. Money issues for couples include excessive spending, disagreements over who controls the money, and not having enough money to meet financial obligations. When one or both of the partners have ADD, these issues become magnified. Arguments about money can affect all aspects of a relationship. If these issues are not resolved, they can lead to permanent damage to the relationship and to your financial standing.

In this chapter and throughout the book, most of the information that relates to couples applies to all couples in intimate relationships, regardless of marital status or gender. The exceptions are those sections that specifically discuss legal issues related to marriage and divorce. The information given also applies whether one or both partners in a relationship have ADD.

HOW ADD AFFECTS RELATIONSHIPS

In general, the ADD population has a higher rate of divorce and remarriage than the non-ADD population (Barkley, Murphy, and Fischer 2008). When people with ADD are married, they may have less marital satisfaction than people without ADD (Eakin et al. 2004) and they report more problems in their marriages than their non-ADD partners (Eakin et al. 2004). Further, partners of people with ADD report more psychological distress and less marital satisfaction than partners of non-ADD people (Minde et al. 2003).

The results from these studies are just as applicable to other partnerships or committed relationships.

When an ADD partner forgets to pay the bills, bounces a check, or spends impulsively, the non-ADD partner may feel like this behavior is due to laziness or apathy, is done intentionally, or is a comment on how little the partner values their relationship. In reality, this forgetful and disorganized behavior is not to be taken personally. People with ADD usually suffer from feelings of guilt and incompetence about their mismanagement of money. And because people with ADD have difficulty learning from their errors, they may still keep making the same mistakes, leading to increased frustration for both partners. Therefore, the issues continue to cause problems—spiraling into more conflict in the relationship.

Your relationship with money is largely based on how your parents handled money when you were a child. Most people learn money management skills from their parents. Because ADD is highly inheritable, it is very likely that one (or even both) of your parents have ADD. If that is the case, you may not have been exposed to good financial practices and may not have learned how to manage your money wisely.

ACTIVITY: Examine Your and Your Partner's History with Money

One way for you and your partner to better understand each other and how each of you handles money is to discuss your earliest experiences with money. You may find that you and your partner had similar experiences or you may find your experiences were totally different. Either way, it opens a window into why you and your partner behave certain ways when it comes to spending and saving money. Discuss the following questions with your partner:

- What is your earliest memory regarding money? Is it a memory of your parents arguing about how much money was being spent? Maybe you remember going with one of your parents to make a deposit at the bank?

- What did you learn about money back then? Did you learn that there would always be enough money for everyone, or did you learn that money was something that was scarce?

- What do you remember the most about your parents' relationship with money?

- Which of your parents' beliefs or attitudes about money do you still carry with you today?

- Are those beliefs helping you or hindering you from achieving financial success?

After discussing these questions with your partner, talk about how you can use these experiences in a positive way—to both decrease the amount of arguing about money and to better understand each other.

Savers and Spenders

In every couple, there is usually a saver and a spender. If given $1,000, the saver will most likely put the money in the bank or invest it, while a spender will go out and buy the large-screen TV he or she has been eyeing. Usually, savers and spenders compliment each other well.

Due to impulsivity, the person with ADD usually falls into the "spender" category. This can lead to marital conflicts regarding excessive spending and increasing debt. However, some people with ADD can be savers because they are keenly aware that they have a tendency to go overboard with their spending. However, being an excessive saver can be just as detrimental as being an excessive spender. Excessive savers run the risk of depriving themselves (and their families) in order to save money. Moderation in saving and spending is the key.

ACTIVITY: What Is Your Spending Style?

You may be a saver, a spender, or a combination of both. This quiz will clarify for you which one you resemble the most.

1. When a new tech gadget comes on the market, I am one of the first to buy it.

   a. Yes

   b. No

2. I have saved up at least two months of living expenses in my savings account.

   a. No

   b. Yes

3. I have had arguments with my partner because I come home from the store with more items than were on the shopping list.

    a. Yes

    b. No

4. Sometimes I deny myself the items I need because I am afraid of running out of money.

    a. No

    b. Yes

5. If I want to make a big purchase, I go home and think about it for a day or two before I buy it.

    a. No

    b. Yes

See how many of your answers are A's and B's. The more A's you have, the more likely it is that you are a spender. You might benefit from paying close attention to where you spend your money and the amount you are spending. If you have more B's, you tend to be a saver. It's great that you are saving up for emergencies, but also make sure you are able to spend money on things that are important to you and your family.

Financial Cheating

People with ADD are more prone to infidelity due to boredom and the need for novelty, and, likewise, they can also be prone to "financial cheating." This includes purposely hiding purchases or accounts from their partner. You may hide purchases because you know your partner is watchful of your impulsive spending and will get angry if he or she finds out about the new purchase. This type of cheating can have just as much of a negative impact on your relationship as having an affair.

One of the exceptions to keeping secret accounts is if you are in an abusive relationship and are planning to leave. In this circumstance, saving money on the side may be a necessity.

ACTIVITY: Issues with Hiding Money

If you are hiding money from your partner, ask yourself the following questions to determine if your secrecy may be hurting your relationship:

- Has your partner shown any abusive behavior (physical, emotional, or sexual)?

- Are you hiding money because otherwise bills won't get paid?

- Does your partner have issues with gambling or compulsive spending?

- Has your partner threatened to cut you off financially if you leave?

- Is your partner addicted to drugs or alcohol?

If you answered yes to one or more of these questions, you may have a justified reason for hiding away money or being secretive about your accounts. If you answered no to all of these questions, you may have discovered that you are hiding money because you have compulsive spending behaviors you want to keep hidden. Counseling is recommended in all of these situations to help you live free of the pressure to hide your money.

Consider Keeping Your Money Separate

There is no rule that states that you have to combine all of your money when you get married. There are a couple of options if you find that having joint accounts is causing conflict in your marriage. One option is to keep your accounts separate. It may be much easier to track your spending habits (and you may have fewer arguments) if you keep separate accounts. You may want to consider having both names on you and your partner's checking accounts, just in case there is an emergency and one of you has to have access to either account to pay bills. Another option is to have a joint account for household expenses and also to keep your own separate accounts.

You can designate which person will pay for utilities, cable, and other fixed costs. Or you can split the bill down the middle, just as roommates do. A helpful rule for figuring out how to divide the mortgage or rent is that each person pays a percentage that is in proportion to their income. If you have a joint credit card, you can split the bill so that each of you pays half or for just the specific items each has purchased. Using individual credit cards is even easier.

Keep in mind that if you jointly apply for credit on a loan, both you and your partner's credit reports may be viewed by a potential lender. This means that if your partner does not pay a bill, even if only his or her name is on that account, it can affect your ability to get the loan, or get a lower interest rate on it. If you open a joint account, shared loan, or have a joint credit card, that information will appear on both of your credit reports.

Some couples may feel that keeping separate accounts decreases their feelings of "togetherness" in the marriage, but consider that keeping your accounts separate may actually increase your ability to stay together happily. And the less you argue about money, the closer you will feel to your partner. If you do divorce, having separate accounts can at least be one less thing to untangle during the divorce process.

Cohabitation and Money

People with ADD tend to have intense relationships that can fade quickly. Part of having an intense relationship can entail impulsive acts—like moving in together soon after the beginning of a relationship. If you are living with a significant other, it is recommended that you keep your finances separate until you have lived together for an extended period of time. This protects you financially and legally.

ACTIVITY: Should You Keep Separate Accounts?

Answer the following questions to better determine if you and your partner should keep separate accounts:

- Are you continually arguing about joint account expenses?

- Have you and/or your partner bounced checks?

- Do you and/or your partner continually forget to record withdrawals from the joint account?

- Do you or your partner have poor credit?

- Are you in a relationship that is not legally binding? (Marriage, common-law marriage, and civil union are legally binding relationships.)

The more questions you answered yes to, the better off you might be if you keep separate accounts. If you try keeping separate accounts, and things get better, then great! If things don't get better, you can always get joint accounts again.

The Setup

Sometimes the non-ADD partner will, intentionally or unintentionally, assign a financial task to the ADD partner that is impossible for the ADD partner to accomplish. There can be a few reasons for this "setup." First, the non-ADD partner may want an opportunity to show the ADD partner once and for all that he really can't handle the finances, thus opening the door for the non-ADD partner to take over. The non-ADD partner may also not be aware of the severity or nature of ADD, erroneously believing that ADD is a result of laziness, not biology, and may hope that giving the ADD partner a financial task can help "straighten him out once and for all." This tactic is rarely, if ever, successful.

Likewise, the ADD partner, intentionally or unintentionally, may not even attempt to begin or complete a financial task. Just as there can be underlying motivations for the non-ADD partner, there may also be some for the ADD partner. The ADD partner may think to himself, "If I really screw up this time, maybe my partner will take over the finances" or "I'll just let this bill go. Ignoring it means I don't have to deal with it." Being aware of these underlying motivations can help you and your partner avoid no-win situations.

ACTIVITY: List Your Money Arguments and Possible Solutions

One of the best ways to diffuse arguments over money is to write out your biggest concerns and then come up with solutions. It sounds deceptively simple, but it is very effective. You are separating the *content* of your argument from the *process*. Sometimes it is easier to write something out than to rehash it over and over again with your partner. This activity is meant to be a springboard for further discussion.

Even if you do not have a partner, you probably have some money arguments with other key people in your life, including your parents, siblings, or boss. This activity applies just as well to those situations.

For this activity and others in the book, it is helpful to have a notebook in which you can write down your responses. A notebook keeps all your information in one place, so it reduces the chances of loose papers getting lost or creating clutter.

For each argument, use the headings listed below to write a sentence in your notebook outlining your point of view about the issue. For example, if you and your partner argue over the cost of day care, your point of view could be, "I think we spend more on day care than we bring in from my partner being at work." Your partner's point of view might be, "I want to work outside the home. I understand day care is expensive, but my job is part of my identity." Possible solutions may include checking out less expensive day care facilities (which may give you a reality check about what you get for your money) or having you and/or your partner ask your supervisor(s) for more flexible work hours, allowing one or both of you to be home more hours a week.

Let yourself come up with many possible solutions—no matter how unrealistic you think they are—because from those "silly" ideas come real solutions.

Issue #1

My view:

My partner's view:

My possible solutions:

My partner's possible solutions:

Issue #2

My view:

My partner's view:

My possible solutions:

My partner's possible solutions:

After you have implemented your solutions, meet again to review how your solutions helped solve the problem. If the solutions did not solve the problem, do this activity again and brainstorm for some new solutions. Remember, there is always the option to agree to disagree.

WAYS TO INCREASE THE WEALTH IN YOUR RELATIONSHIP

Money is just one of the many ingredients or issues in a marriage or partnership. But it is an essential one. There are quite a few ways to improve the financial strain in your relationship. Each solution requires varying degrees of involvement. What works for one couple may not work for another—try out what feels right, and if it doesn't work, move on to the next option.

Here are some suggestions for improving your relationship's wealth—and not just in the financial sense.

Talk About Money Up Front

Having similar views about money is a key factor in any successful marriage (Bernard 2008). In an ideal world, couples should discuss their financial goals and standing before getting married (Bernard 2008). Do you want to have children? Do you plan on working immediately after children? If so, who will care for the children during the day, and who will pay for this? Do you have any debt you have not disclosed to your partner? Do you have a good credit history? Would you be willing to relocate if you or your partner were offered a better job? When do you want to retire? Even if you are already married, it's never too late to find out the answers to these questions.

Don't Expect Your Partner to Change

Sometimes people get married with the intention of converting their partner into someone less messy or impulsive or talkative or compulsive or whatever. If you marry someone with the expectation that you can change him or her, you are setting yourself up for failure.

Keep in mind that the things that you may want to "fix" about your partner also have a positive side as well. For example, it may irritate you that your wife loans out money to her relatives; However, she is generous and you may appreciate her dedication to her family. There is a flip side to everything. It all depends on whether the benefits of the relationship (such as having a generous partner) are worth the risks (loaning out money you don't necessarily have). Only you can make that decision.

Meet Every Week for a Financial Check-In

It is important to keep each other informed of any large purchases, bills, or upcoming financial requirements. Meeting every week, even for a brief period of time, can prevent issues from blowing up into an argument. The meeting does not have to be long—even fifteen minutes will suffice. Sometimes just bringing the topic out in the open helps create a solution. Just stick with topics that you feel are resolvable without outside intervention.

Come to the meeting prepared—write down any issues beforehand that you would like to discuss. It helps to pick the most important issue on your list so that you can have just one focus during the meeting and be more likely to stay on topic. Issues couples might discuss during this meeting include the purchase of an expensive item, an overdue bill, wanting to save more money for retirement, or how much to spend on holiday gifts.

A helpful guideline is to have one partner bring up a topic and then spend five minutes talking about his or her concerns. Set a timer so you keep moving along. Then the other partner talks for five minutes about his or her concerns. Keep your concerns factual and not emotional. For example, a factual concern would be one based on numbers or written proof, such as, "Our cell phone bill was $100 more this month because you went over your text-message limit." An example of an emotional response would be, "You screwed up again! You cost us so much money because once again you were irresponsible!" It is much more productive when you stick to the facts rather than make an emotional plea or criticism. This is easier said than done, but it will result in a much more productive resolution.

If the discussion starts getting heated, or if you feel your emotions starting to bubble up, here are some ways you can avoid a fight:

- Be aware of the signals your body gives you when you are getting upset. It can be difficult for people with ADD to be aware of these signals. They include an increased heart rate, feeling flushed, and hand tremors.

- Take deep breaths.

- Remember that in the scheme of life, this is not a big deal.

- Count to 10 (or to 25 if you have ADD).

- If you feel verbally attacked, calmly tell your partner that you are feeling uncomfortable and that you need to talk about the issue more calmly.

■ Tell your partner that you need to take a break for fifteen minutes. Then walk away. Make sure you come back after the fifteen minutes are up.

The last five minutes of the meeting should be used to find a win-win solution—one in which each partner benefits. For example, you bring up the issue that you are concerned the TV your partner purchased is too expensive. A win-win solution would be to sell unwanted items in your house in a garage sale or online to get some extra cash for the TV. This way your partner can keep the TV, and you get rid of stuff you no longer need. If you cannot solve the issue within the fifteen minutes, table it and talk about it in a couple of days.

Sometimes a win-win solution is not within reach. In this case, you may need to compromise with your partner. This means that you may need to let go of how you want your issue to be resolved. It helps to have a clear idea of what you are willing to compromise on and what you will not bend on. For example, using the TV issue discussed above, you may decide that you are willing to keep the TV only if you and your partner find a way to get some extra money to pay for the TV. You may also decide that you will not budge on having the TV returned if you will not be able to pay some of your bills that month. If you find that an issue is not resolvable, you can decide to either let the issue remain unresolved, or seek the advice of a financial professional or a counselor.

MONEY ARGUMENTS

When engaged in a battle of wills, it is important to look at the *content* of the argument versus the *process*. While a couple's biggest argument may be that the ADD partner spends money the couple does not have (content), it is important to look at how that argument usually plays out (process). Relationships are like a dance. Who makes the first move toward an argument? Who ends the argument? Who *has to* end the argument, at all costs? Sometimes, you may notice that the argument isn't about money at all—it is more about who has control of what in the relationship.

You may want to ask yourself, "What is this argument *really* about? Is it bringing up some past issues for me?" When your partner tells you that he feels you are charging too much on your credit card, does it remind you of your parents arguing about money? Is your partner really being unreasonable or is he just reminding you of the arguing in your past relationships? Sometimes just realizing that you are really upset about something from your past can help you discuss a topic with your partner instead of getting into an argument. You may even want to tell your partner that talking about a certain issue brings up bad feelings for you because of past experiences.

You can also ask your partner in a calm voice, "What are you needing from me right now?" You may find the answer surprising. It may have nothing to do with the topic at hand. For example, you are arguing with your partner because she feels you are not being open about what you are spending money on. If you ask, "What are you needing from me right now?" you may get the response that she would like to feel more needed by you and would like you to share more with her.

Put the Non-ADD Person in Charge

If there is a non-ADD person in the relationship, you might consider putting this person in charge of paying the bills and keeping track of the money. This should be a decision made by both you and your partner together. "Keeping track of the money" includes writing checks, paying bills, and setting up online deposits and withdrawals. It includes all the detail work that is a challenge for people with ADD.

In some cases, you may find that you (the ADD partner) are better at financial management than your non-ADD partner. That is okay, too— whoever is better at keeping track of money should pay the bills and write the checks.

In some cases, the person who is put in charge of the money can use it as a way to wield power in the relationship. This behavior is usually not related to money specifically and is probably a pattern of control in other areas of your relationship. This type of control is worth examining with a counselor.

Even if you have difficulty with money management, you should still have an equal say in how your money is spent. This applies even if you are a stay-at-home parent and do not receive an income. Marriage is a partnership—and in business partnerships, each partner has an equal say. Why should your marriage be any different? When you don't have an equal say in your marriage, it can lead to building anger and frustration.

You can have your partner take over the day-to-day financial workings of your home, like writing checks and paying bills, while still having an equal say in what items are being purchased, how your money is being spent, and other concerns, if any, about money issues.

Hiring Someone to Help

What do you do if you both have ADD? You may greatly benefit from hiring an assistant to help you with these day-to-day tasks. (You will learn more about hiring an assistant in chapter 5.)

Another option is to delegate your money management to a professional. While you may think hiring a professional will cost you too much money, it may actually save you money (and may improve your relationship) in the long run. It is important to find the right financial professional for you, matching your needs both in services provided and in your comfort level with the person. In chapter 4, you will learn about the different types of money management professionals and their credentials.

SEEKING COUNSELING

If money issues are causing problems in your relationship, consider couples counseling. There are licensed counselors who specialize in working with couples. You can find these counselors by using an online directory or phone book or by getting a referral from trusted family or friends. See the Resources section at the end of this book for information on locating a couples therapist.

When you contact a counselor, ask if he or she has experience with helping adults with ADD. It is usually better if both partners attend counseling. This is not only because you are both in the relationship, but also because people with ADD often have difficulties with self-awareness. They may not recognize the severity of their ADD symptoms and also may not fully realize the impact of their behavior on others (Knouse et al. 2005). Therefore, having both of you at the counseling appointment is very beneficial to your relationship.

If your partner refuses to attend counseling sessions, go on your own. You can still benefit. Be aware, however, that when one of you changes the dynamic of the relationship, the entire relationship will change. This change can lead to an improved relationship, or it can lead to one person finding that he or she can no longer function in the relationship—he or she has outgrown it, realized it is not a healthy relationship, or come to terms with the fact that the relationship has run its course. If you decide to attend counseling, be aware that you are making a decision that will create some discomfort in the relationship, at least at first, and that change is inevitable.

Things a Counselor Might Ask

If the counselor is familiar with ADD, he or she may ask you about your symptoms. For example, he or she may ask whether you are more hyperactive or inattentive. The counselor may also ask both of you about your main concerns or issues. If money is a major issue in your relationship, the counselor may ask who is in charge of what: Who pays the bills? Do both of you work, or is one of you a stay-at-home parent? What is the biggest frustration for each of you?

Keep in mind that counseling is not a cure-all for your relationship issues. Counseling is like a lot of other things in life—you get out of it what you put into it. If you feel that you do not "click" with a counselor, there are others to choose from. If you feel that the counselor is biased toward one of you, point that out. Good counselors will appreciate that feedback.

ACTIVITY: Determine Your Main Money Issues in Your Relationship

If you have ADD, you may have so many things running through your mind at the therapy session that it may be a challenge to remember your main concerns. Before you even go to your first therapy session, it is helpful to narrow down the issues that most concern you about money and your relationship. For the exercise in this book, you should get an ordinary, ruled notebook. In your notebook, write down your top three concerns, chosen from the list below. Also feel free to add a concern that might not be listed here. You can then bring your notebook to your therapy session.

Money Issues That Might Be Affecting Your Relationship

Credit card debt	Gambling	Lack of savings
"Sneaky" spending	Bounced checks	Loans
Poor credit rating	Disorganized paperwork	Late bills
Control of money	Excessive spending	Child support
Bankruptcy	Lack of communication about spending	

Now that you have picked your top three concerns, it will be easier to stay on track during your therapy session.

THE LAST RESORT

If you feel that your marriage is damaged beyond repair, there is the option of divorce. Do not take this step lightly, however, because it costs you emotionally and financially. Not only do you and your children experience the loss of the marriage and family, but you may also experience a less-than-amicable divorce, resulting in increased legal fees and increased stress. When making this important decision, look at whether you are hurting yourself and your children more by staying in the marriage. In chapter 2, you will learn more about the financial ramifications of divorce and how to protect yourself financially during that time.

SUMMARY

In this chapter, you learned about financial issues that are specific to couples wherein one or both of the partners have ADD. You also learned about solutions to these issues, such as having a "financial check-in" with your partner and seeking counseling. In the next chapter, you will learn how specific life events such as marriage, children, and divorce affect your financial outlook. You will also learn how to protect yourself financially in these situations.

CHAPTER 2

Life Issues and Money

Many people experience life events such as marrying, having children, divorcing, and becoming disabled. However, people with ADD are more likely to experience some of these events. People with ADD have a higher rate of divorce than the non-ADD population (Biederman, Faraone, et al. 2006). They are also more likely to have unplanned pregnancies than the non-ADD population (Barkley, Murphy, and Fischer 2008) and more likely to have injuries than the non-ADD population (Swensen et al. 2004). In this chapter, you will learn how major life transitions affect your finances, and you will also learn how to lessen the financial impact of these events.

MARRIAGE AND WEDDINGS

In the United States, the average wedding costs $23,657 (Smart Money 2008). Because people with ADD have a habit of "snowball spending"—getting carried away and going way over budget—a wedding can wind up costing you a lot of money. Remember that the whole purpose of a wedding is to have your family and friends come together to support and bless your marriage. The purpose is not to throw the best party *ever*. In fact, you may find that friends who threw a less expensive wedding had a better time than those who spent a lot of money.

Reducing the Cost of Your Wedding

You don't want to start your new married life returning to a pile of debt after your honeymoon. Here are some ways to cut your wedding costs.

- **Get married off-season:** Wedding season usually occurs from May to October. If you get married during one of the off-peak months, you will not only save money but will also have a wider selection of venues. You will probably have a cheaper honeymoon too.

- **Get married on a different day:** The most expensive time for renting a reception hall is on a Saturday night, due to demand. Schedule your wedding for Friday night or Sunday instead. If you have ADD, you are probably used to doing things a little differently than everyone else, so why not have a wedding on a different day?

- **Slim down the cake:** Get a smaller version of the wedding cake you want and have a sheet cake hidden in the back that you can serve your guests. You may also consider having a more basic cake than you originally envisioned. You can still have a beautiful cake even if it doesn't have all of the extras. You can also order your cake from your local culinary arts school or from your supermarket.

- **Get a less expensive gown:** You only wear your wedding gown once, and most people don't remember your dress anyway, so buy a less expensive gown. You can find brand-new dresses online. Another money-saving tip is to always buy your dress one or two sizes larger than what you would normally wear. You can always have a dress altered to be smaller, but you usually can't alter a dress to make it bigger. Some brides have taken the route of renting their wedding dress. Just be aware that you cannot make any alterations to a rented dress.

- **Have a smaller wedding party:** When your wedding party consists of just a maid of honor and best man, there are fewer bridesmaid dresses to buy, fewer tuxes to rent, and less hassle. If your friends ask you why they weren't picked as your brides-maids, you can just blame the bad economy. You can still have your friends play big roles in your wedding ceremony, such as being a reader or usher, or carrying the rings.

- **Scale back on your invitations:** Do you really need calligraphy on the envelopes? People just throw those out anyway. You can have custom-made invitations printed at an office supply store on nice cardstock (thick paper) and have them cut to fit in a regular envelope. This reduces the cost of envelopes and postage. You can ask a creative friend or family member to design artwork for your invitation. This way you can create a unique invitation that will probably look better and be more personalized than anything you could order from a catalog. Some couples even print out their wedding invitations on home computers.

- **Rethink your reception:** Have the reception in the same location as your ceremony. Then you are paying for one location only, not two. Your guests will probably appreciate staying in one location rather than driving across town for your reception. It's also much easier to plan and organize a wedding ceremony and reception when they are held at the same location. Ask your friends or members of your family to help you. The more people pitching in with planning and organizing, the better!

- **Have a smaller ceremony:** Many couples get married in a very small ceremony and then invite their family and friends to a reception either immediately afterward or even up to weeks later. Before you take this option, make sure this will go over well with your family and friends. You don't want to start your marriage off with angry and disappointed parents and in-laws.

- **Honeymoon close to home:** Honeymoon in a nearby location. This doesn't mean you have to stay in the motel down the street—any local place that doesn't necessitate airfare usually brings honeymoon costs down. If you honeymoon locally, you also won't have to deal with all the hassles of packing and then flying immediately after your wedding.

Remember, very few (if any) people remember your invitations, reception hall, cake, or any other part of your wedding. Think of the money you are saving and how you will now be able to put that money down toward a house or your future children's college tuition (but we all know they are going to get full scholarships, right?).

Prenuptial and Postnuptial Agreements

A *prenuptial agreement* is an agreement signed before you get married. It details how your assets will be separated and what alimony should be paid if you and your spouse get divorced. A *postnuptial agreement* is the same type of agreement, but it is signed after you get married. You may feel that having an agreement like this is not a very romantic thing to do right before or after you get married. But fighting over your assets if you get divorced isn't very romantic either. Prenuptial and postnuptial agreements can greatly reduce disputes over money and property. And considering that people with ADD get divorced (and remarried) more than the general population, a pre- or postnuptial agreement might be a good idea. Prenuptial and postnuptial agreements must be written in a very specific way, so make sure you consult an attorney.

ACTIVITY: Keep Track of Your Wedding Expenses

Wedding expenses can start spiraling out of control whether you have ADD or not. But keeping track of those expenses can be a real challenge for people with ADD. Add the following list to your notebook to keep track of what you are paying to whom. With the excitement of planning a wedding, it can be easy to forget something. Now you will be able to see, way ahead of time, what you are missing. You can also use this list to compare the cost of different vendors, such as florists and caterers.

Item	Dollar Amount
Invitations	_____
Postage	_____
Ceremony location fee	_____
Clergy fee	_____
Bridal dress	_____
Bridal accessories	_____
Bridesmaids' dresses	_____
Bridesmaids' accessories	_____

Tux rentals   _____

Flowers   _____

Reception venue fee   _____

Catering   _____

Cake   _____

Alcohol/beverages   _____

Favors for guests   _____

Other expenses   _____

_____

_____

_____

_____

Total   _____

Once you have come up with your total, compare it to how much money you have to spend. This includes money you and your future spouse have saved up, plus any monetary gifts from each of your parents. You should pay these expenses with money you have in the bank and use your credit cards as little as possible.

If you find that your total amount exceeds the money you have to work with, look at areas where you may be able to scale back. Maybe you can get invitations that use regular-size envelopes so you don't have to pay extra postage on larger envelopes. Little changes like that add up to big savings!

CHILDREN

People with ADD have a ten times higher rate of unexpected pregnancy than people who do not have ADD. (Barkley, Murphy, and Fischer 2008). This may be due to not using birth control consistently, if at all. Birth control costs a lot less than raising a child. If you are having difficulties maintaining your birth control, talk to your doctor about a more easily managed option.

Having a child before you are financially ready increases your stress level, which can, in turn, affect your baby's development. Unexpected pregnancies can also put a strain on what may be an already fragile relationship. Today the cost of raising a child through the age of seventeen can run up to $250,000 (U.S. Department of Agriculture 2007). This does not include college costs or any costs for children over the age of eighteen, but if you think the costs end when your child turns eighteen, think again. Ask any parent of a college student, and they will tell you otherwise. For the 2008–2009 academic year, the yearly tuition for a private four-year college averaged $25,143 a year. A public four-year school averaged $6,585 a year. That was a 6 percent increase from the previous year (College Board 2008). Even if your child is on full scholarship, there are still costs involved. You will learn more about saving up for college in chapter 10.

Managing Expenses with a Baby

Babies are very expensive, especially once you add up the costs of food, formula, and diapers, not to mention all the other accessories babies need. There are various ways you can reduce the costs of having a baby.

BORROW ITEMS

Babies grow out of clothes quickly. A simple solution to saving money on clothes is to borrow them from other parents. You can also go to a children's consignment store. Some children's clothing at consignment stores will still have the tags attached because the babies grew so quickly that the items could never be worn!

Important: Older cribs may have slats that are too far apart, making it possible for a baby to get his or her head caught between the slats. Newer cribs have appropriately placed slats that are narrowly spaced so it is impossible for a baby to poke his or her head out between them.

SAFETY ITEMS

If you have ADD, there is an increased chance that your child may also have ADD. ADD children tend to be more active than other children and have an uncanny ability to get into whatever is off limits. If you have a swimming pool, it is imperative that you have some type of alarm system and/or gate around it. If you have a gate, make sure it is locked at all times. You also want to make sure you have safety latches on all the cabinets within your child's reach. In addition, get a latch that locks the toilet lid down when not in use. Baby-proofing your house is well worth any additional cost to you.

MEDICAL INSURANCE FOR CHILDREN

If you have health insurance, your child can be added to your policy as a dependent. If you do not have health insurance, all states have state-sponsored health insurance programs specifically created for children. While each state's rules for qualifying differ, most require that the child be under eighteen years old and that the family make less than a specific annual income. In many cases, both parents can be working and still qualify for the insurance. Some states even allow you to apply for coverage for your unborn child. For more information on your state's health insurance program for children, see the Resources section at the end of this book.

GOVERNMENT AID PROGRAMS

In the United States, there are federal and state programs available if you are living at the poverty level and have a child under the age of five. These programs provide assistance with food and formula, and they may also provide other needed services for young children. There are also other governmental aid programs available for housing and medical care if you meet poverty guidelines. For more information on government aid, see the Resources section at the end of this book.

FINDING DAY CARE

Due to the costs of day care, you may find that it actually saves you more money to stay at home with your child than to go to work. You can check if a trusted friend or family member will watch your child, or you can check with your employer to see if he or she will allow you to do *flextime* (whereby you work part time and share your job duties with someone else). You can also see if your employer will let you telecommute by working from home. Keep in mind, though, that when you have ADD, it can be a challenge to work from home because of the increased distractions.

ACTIVITY: Researching the Cost of Day Care

To help determine if day care is a good option for you, first ask yourself if your child is emotionally ready for day care. If so, answer the following questions in your notebook:

- Do you need full-time or part-time day care?

- How much money can you afford per week for day care?

- Can you afford to have in-home day care?

- Will the money you make at work exceed the money you plan to spend on day care?

- Do you qualify for any extra assistance with day care costs?

- Is there a trusted family member who is willing to provide care for your child?

When visiting a day care, make an unscheduled visit—just drop in. You want to see the day care as it normally runs during the day. Ask the day care director the following questions and record this in your notebook also:

- What are your hours of operation?

- What is the rate of staff turnover?

- Are the day care teachers certified in early childhood development?

- What are your fees?

- What exactly is included in the fees?

- What other expenses are there (field trips, extra activities, uniforms)?

- If there is an extra fee associated with an activity, and I am unable to pay that fee, what will my child be doing during that time?

- If my child gets sick or we take a vacation, is my fee prorated (reduced)?

- Are there late fees if I don't pick up my child by a certain time?

In addition to these questions, ask to see the day care's license and any certifications. Also ask other parents for their opinions on day cares in your community. Word-of-mouth referrals are very valuable indicators of the quality of a day care center. If you feel hesitant about the day cares you visited, it is best to wait until you find one with which you feel comfortable.

Children with Special Needs

Many parents of special needs children are concerned about how their children will be taken care of after both parents' deaths. In particular there is a concern that a child will no longer qualify for Social Security benefits if he or she inherits assets from parents.

A *special needs trust* allows a person with disabilities to continue to get Social Security benefits even after parents die and leave him or her money. Owning a car, house, or other tangible goods does not affect eligibility for Social Security benefits, but money in a bank account can. That's why money that normally would be inherited by your child would instead be held in the trust.

So how does the money come out of the trust? You appoint a trustee who disburses the money in the trust in the event of your death. It is recommended that the trustee you select be someone with good money management skills who has your child's best interests and welfare as a priority. The trustee can be someone in your family, a close friend, a financial adviser, or your attorney.

A trustee can use the money in the trust to buy tangible items like a computer or car for your child. The trustee can't give money directly to your child because that would affect eligibility for Social Security benefits.

An alternative to a special needs trust is a *pooled trust* or *community trust*. These trusts are managed by nonprofit organizations, and they hold funds for several families at a time. Talk to other parents of special needs children or to special needs organizations for recommendations on attorneys and pooled trusts. For more information on special needs trusts, see the Resources section at the end of this book.

DIVORCE

As you learned earlier, people with ADD are more likely to divorce than people without ADD. You may have thought getting married cost a lot of money; divorce will cost you much more, financially and emotionally.

Ways to Save Money on Your Divorce

Divorce will cost you, no matter what, but there are a few ways you can get divorced with as minimal an effect on your pocketbook as can be managed.

FIND THE RIGHT ATTORNEY FOR YOU

Get recommendations from friends and family members to find the right attorney for your needs. Paying a little more for a good attorney may save you money in the long run. Also make sure that the attorney specializes in family law, particularly divorce law. You can also contact your state's bar association to see if it certifies attorneys in family or divorce law and if so, if someone can refer you to a few in your local area. Also make sure you are comfortable with your attorney's level of legal aggressiveness. Ideally you will not need an adversarial attorney, and being excessively adversarial may cost you more money.

USE THE SAME ATTORNEY

If you have limited shared assets and you agree on the terms of the divorce, you and your spouse may be able to use the same attorney. You can always have another attorney look over the documents before you file them.

LET STUFF GO

When you are going through a divorce, it is important to let stuff go. But this doesn't just apply to emotional stuff—it includes stuff in your house too. Fighting over certain items in your home can wind up costing you a lot more money than the items are worth. Do you really want that green lampshade, or is it that you are having difficulty letting go of your former marriage and spouse? You may also notice that your ADD and impulsivity may give you a knee-jerk reaction of "I need all of this stuff!" Remember, it's just that—stuff. Transition and change are difficult for people with ADD, but remember that having more stuff doesn't make the transition or change "go away" any faster. You might as well have less stuff, since being surrounded by clutter (especially clutter from your marital home) can hinder your thinking (and healing) process.

If you are finding that you just cannot let things go and it is affecting your ability to move through the divorce process, it is recommended that you talk with a counselor. Divorce is a very stressful life event and can be even more stressful than a spouse's death. For other resources on divorce, see the Resources section at the end of this book.

SETTLE THINGS ON YOUR OWN

Whether they realize it or not, some divorcing spouses prolong squabbling over items and dollar amounts so that they can continue to have contact with each other. Also, when you have ADD, impulsivity can lead to increased incidences of saying things you don't mean and taking actions that are not in your best interest. So make a concerted effort to conduct yourself with as much integrity and class as possible during the settlement process.

The divorce process varies from state to state, so it is recommended that you contact an attorney. Having an attorney also helps make it more possible to have a "fair" split of assets. If you can't afford an attorney, don't have any assets to divide, or would just prefer not to work with an attorney, most courthouses have family law clinics where an adviser helps you fill out forms and explains the legal process to you. This service varies from county to county. Contact your county's courthouse for more information.

CHECK YOUR BILLS

During the separation and divorce process, review your bills to make sure that your estranged spouse has not seriously increased his or her spending. If you have a joint credit card with your spouse, your spouse is still legally able to use that card until you remove his or her name from the account. You may have to close the account and reopen another just in your name. See your credit card issuer for details. If your spouse has charged several items to this credit card, you may not be responsible for some (or possibly all) of the charges if it is so stated in your separation agreement. If you are on civil terms with your spouse, try talking about the charges first. If you have an acrimonious relationship, seek advice from your attorney or an accountant.

HAVE ALL OF YOUR DOCUMENTS TOGETHER

Attorneys charge in *billable hours*. That means you are paying for every minute you meet with your attorney. Getting all your documents and questions together ahead of time can help keep costs down, but this is also a particular challenge for people who have ADD. If you are unsure about what documents to bring with you to an appointment, ask your attorney ahead of time. You can also have a friend or family member, specifically someone who is organized and has been through the divorce process, review your documents and list of questions to make sure you haven't missed anything.

ACTIVITY: Document Checklist for Meeting with Your Attorney

It can be hard enough keeping track of papers when you have ADD. And this is a time when you really need to have all your important financial documents together—leaving something out can mean a change in the outcome of your divorce settlement. Copy the following checklist into your notebook and use it to get started on collecting everything you'll need when you are at the attorney's office. This is a partial list, so it is recommended that you call the attorney to confirm exactly what you need to bring to the appointment. Add to the list in your notebook during this conversation.

Income tax returns (personal)

Income tax returns (business—if you are self-employed)

Personal bank account statements

Spouse bank account statements

Joint bank account statements

Mortgage statements

Mortgage refinancing paperwork

Documents with the legal description of any real estate you own

Any life insurance policies on you, your spouse, or your children

A list of any debts, including loans and credit card debt

Any statements from retirement accounts

Titles and registrations from any vehicles you own

Note that you should bring your income tax records from the past three years. It's understandable that you may not have access to your spouse's records. That is okay—it's more important that you have all of your own documents.

DISABILITY

Other than having disability insurance and a living will (which you'll learn more about in chapter 3), there is not much you can do to prepare for most disabilities. However, one exception would be if you were to become incapacitated or otherwise could not make decisions about your medical treatment. Consider the possibility that during your disability you could have a caregiver attend to your medical matters through a health care surrogacy, and could have your legal and financial matters handled through a power of attorney.

Giving someone *power of attorney* means that he or she may have access to your bank accounts and can pay your bills or even sell your property. If you do name someone to act with power of attorney in the event that you are incapacitated, make sure it is a close relative or trusted friend or adviser. A *health care surrogate* can make medical decisions on your behalf if you are incapacitated, such as agreeing to remove you from life support, but a health care surrogate would not be able to take care of your legal and financial matters like someone who has power of attorney.

If you want to name a surrogate, you can download forms for your state online (see "Health Care Surrogate Forms" in the Resources section at the end of this book). Fill the forms out as instructed and sign two originals—one for you to keep and another for your surrogate to hold. For your bank and/or brokerage accounts, you will likely have to fill out a specific form required by that bank or *brokerage* (a company that allows you to buy or sell stock and other investments). Call or visit the bank or brokerage and ask what the process is for you to give someone power of attorney for your account. If you want to give someone general power of attorney for all of your assets and properties, you should consult an attorney so that he or she can draft a power of attorney form that meets your needs. Keep a copy of any power of attorney forms you sign with your other important papers. Note that a power of attorney is only valid while you are alive.

DEATH

In the event of your death, it is important that your family can quickly find important documents. This includes your bank account records, tax records, and will. You can have a friend help you organize this information. Since the originals of these items may be filed in several different folders, you may want to keep photocopies of these items together in their own folder so that your family has easy access to this information. You can learn more about wills in chapter 3, and you can learn more about organizing your financial papers in chapter 5.

It's a good idea to tell your family members your preferred funeral plans and to put these plans in writing. This is one less thing for your family to think about. And it also helps family members avoid conflicts (such as when one relative wants "Wind Beneath My Wings" played at your funeral and another wants "Purple People Eater").

When someone dies, there are financial concerns that arise, such as the cost of the funeral. Since bank accounts may not be accessible after your death, it is recommended that your spouse or adult child have a credit card in his or her name so that if funds are not available, expenses can be charged.

Many states allow you to designate a *beneficiary* (someone you have selected to receive the money) for your current bank accounts. Accounts with beneficiaries are sometimes referred to as *in trust for* (ITF) or *payable-on-death* (POD) accounts. When you die, the money in your account then transfers to your beneficiary. Designating a beneficiary for your bank accounts is a good idea, especially if you want to avoid *probate* (a legal process in which a judge distributes your assets to heirs) or if you want someone to be able to pay bills after your death and until probate starts. To access the money, your beneficiary must present a death certificate to the bank. Many brokerages offer this feature as well.

WINDFALLS

A *windfall* occurs when you receive a large, unexpected amount of money. You may think that acquiring a large amount of money would solve your financial woes and make you happier. However, consider that many people who win the lottery find that their lives actually take a turn for the worse. One-third of lottery winners file for bankruptcy within five years of winning (Kirk and Young 2007). While that may make you feel better about never winning the lottery, it brings up an important point. If you receive a large (and unexpected) amount of money, contact an attorney, financial adviser, and/or accountant before you spend any of the money. This is especially important advice for people with ADD because they have a tendency to spend money more intensely when they know there is a lot available.

ACTIVITY: Make a Financial Time Line

Events in your life may have had more of a financial impact on you than you have realized. Get your notebook and turn it lengthwise. Draw a line from the center of the left edge to the center of the right edge of the paper. This is your life's time line. The beginning of the line is your birth, and the end of the line is the present time. At the points when you had major life events—you graduated from college, got your first job, got married, had children, got divorced, and so on—put a dot either below or above the line relative to how the event impacted your finances, and then label that dot with the corresponding life event. A dot below the line means that this event caused you financial stress or difficulties. A dot above the line means that this event had a positive impact on your finances. If you remember an event that had a particularly intense impact on you, make that dot or point higher or lower than the others. For example, graduating from college may be a dot below the line because at that time you were looking for a job and thinking about all the money you owed in student loans. You may have a dot way above the line for when you got your first job after college because it meant you could make your student loan payments!

Now connect the dots with one continuous line. Are you surprised by what you see? You may be having financial difficulties now, but can you see a time earlier in your life when you were having financial difficulties and you were able to pull yourself out of them? When you have ADD, it can be easy to forget your successes. You may now see from your time line that you have had financial success in the past. Also notice your pattern of financial ups and downs. Everyone has them. Note if your time line looks like a really intense rollercoaster. What made the highs so high? What made the lows so low? The goal is to get to a place where your time line has more ups than downs, and the downs aren't too far below that line.

SUMMARY

In this chapter, you learned how life events that are important, like marriage, divorce, children, disability, death, and windfalls, can affect your financial standing. You also learned how to decrease the financial impact of these events. In the next chapter, you will learn how to save up for your retirement.

CHAPTER 3

Planning for Your Future

How do people with ADD plan for their retirement? They don't, not usually, anyway. ADD is a result of impairment of the executive functions of the brain, as you learned in this book's introduction. One of these executive functions is planning. This means that it may be difficult for you to look ahead and see that you will be retiring someday. Unless you have a money tree in your backyard (and wouldn't that be nice), you will need to start saving up. If you are planning to retire at sixty-two and your life expectancy is eighty-five, you need to have at least twenty-three years worth of living expenses saved up, including enough money for rent or mortgage. This chapter will show you how to have enough money to provide for your needs after you retire.

Consider planning for your retirement to be a kind of insurance policy that you will be financially secure when the time comes, not only to meet your living expenses but also to have an active and exciting postwork life. And just like the commercials for life insurance say, saving for your retirement isn't just for you; it's also for your family.

TYPES OF RETIREMENT ACCOUNTS

There are two main types of retirement accounts: those an individual sets up, such as the Individual Retirement Account (IRA), and those an employer sets up, such as the 401(k) and Simplified Employee Pension IRA (SEP IRA). Your employer is not legally required to offer you a retirement account. Because retirement accounts minimize taxes, you may want to contribute as much money as possible each year. If you have your employer automatically put the maximum amount in your retirement account each pay period, you may not even notice that that money is missing from your paycheck. You will just plan your budget based on the amount of money you have left. (See chapter 6 for details on how to budget.)

Individual Retirement Account (IRA)

There are two types of individual IRAs: traditional and Roth. The biggest difference between the two is that the traditional IRA is tax deferred and the Roth IRA is not:

- The money you put into a *traditional IRA* is usually *tax deductible*—that is, some or all of the money you put in a traditional IRA is deducted from your income on your tax return—as long as your annual income level doesn't exceed a certain amount. Because you can take a tax deduction for the money you put into a traditional IRA, you have to pay taxes on some or all of the money you withdraw.

- *Roth IRAs* have a maximum income limit—if you earn over a certain amount of money one year, you can't contribute to your Roth IRA that year. If your income approaches or is at six figures, see your financial adviser. Contributions to a Roth IRA are not tax deductible, but when you withdraw money, it will be tax free. This is one of the great advantages of the Roth IRA.

There is a restriction on how much you can contribute to your IRA each calendar year. In 2009, the maximum annual amount was $5,000 if you were under age fifty, and $6,000 if you were fifty or over. You can contribute anytime during the calendar year and even up until April 15 of the next year. You can deposit the money in one lump sum or you can contribute a little at a time. Keep in mind that if you do not meet the maximum contribution by April 15, you are not able to tack the remaining amount onto next year's maximum. For example, if you have a maximum annual amount of $5,000 but put only $3,000 in your IRA this year, you cannot put a total of $7,000 in the next year.

Once the money is in your IRA, the money can be invested in a variety of ways, including purchasing stock, mutual funds, CDs, or bonds. For more information on investing, see chapter 4. If you take money out of your

IRA before you turn 59½ years old, you will pay a penalty of 10 percent in addition to your normal income taxes on the amount you take out. You must start withdrawing the money in your IRA by age 70½ or pay a tax.

If you take a tax deduction for each traditional IRA contribution you make, then you pay taxes on 100 percent of the withdrawals when you retire. If you take no deductions or partial deductions, you need to fill out an IRS worksheet to figure out your taxes. It is important to keep track of how much you contribute to your traditional IRA each year and keep the statements showing your contributions. These are papers you just have to hold on to. Seek the advice of a financial professional if you have questions about traditional or Roth IRAs.

Simplified Employee Pension IRA (SEP IRA)

Under a SEP IRA, an employer makes a contribution to your traditional IRA and you do not pay any taxes on those contributions until you withdraw money from that IRA. You can have a percentage of your *net income* (which is what is left after taxes are taken out) contributed, up to a certain dollar amount. SEP IRAs are used mostly by small businesses and the self-employed. To set up a SEP IRA, you need the assistance of a financial adviser.

401(k)

With a 401(k), you transfer part of your paycheck into a retirement account set up through your employer. Your employer has the option to make a contribution as well. If you change jobs, you can move the money into your new employer's 401(k) account or you can move the money into a special IRA called a *rollover IRA*. You can then either keep the money in your rollover IRA, move it to a traditional or Roth IRA, or you can move it to your new employer's 401(k). There are different types of 401(k), depending on your profession. Ask your employer for more information.

SOCIAL SECURITY

When people refer to "Social Security," they usually mean the payments the U.S. government provides for retirees over the age of sixty-five, the disabled, and surviving children and spouses. When you look at your paycheck and stub, you can see your contribution to Social Security under "FICA" (the Federal Insurance Contributions Act, which funds Social Security).

In the future, there may be less Social Security benefits to go around due to the large increase in the number of people who are reaching retirement age. With this increasing burden on the Social Security system, the pie may be divided into smaller and smaller pieces. It would be wise not to count on Social Security to provide you with a majority of your retirement income. In fact, to be on the safe side, count on paying for 100 percent of your basic living expenses with your own retirement savings. For more information on Social Security benefits, see the Resources section at the end of this book.

INSURANCE

Most insurance policies work by giving you a dollar amount (*benefit*) when certain events, defined in your policy, happen. To get this money or benefit, you need to make periodic payments, called *premiums*, to the insurance company. In this section, you will learn about health, catastrophic medical, life, and disability insurance.

Health Insurance

Because medical costs are higher for people with ADD, it is imperative that you have health insurance (Swensen et al. 2004). With today's economy, however, getting health insurance and being able to pay for it are much easier said than done. Try not to have a lapse in your health insurance coverage. If you do have a lapse in your coverage, an insurance company may not cover any *preexisting conditions* (medical issues and diagnoses that you had prior to obtaining your current policy).

HOW TO GET HEALTH INSURANCE

The first place to look for medical insurance is through your employer. If your employer has a group policy, the insurance may still pay for treatment of preexisting conditions. It is also usually less expensive for you to join your employer's group policy than to purchase an individual policy.

If your employer does not offer insurance or if you are self-employed or unemployed, you have a few options. You can obtain an individual plan through an insurance agent. Your premium may be higher than with group health insurance plans, and individual plans may not cover some (or any) of the costs associated with your preexisting conditions. You may also qualify for a federal, state, or local health insurance program. See chapter 2 for information on health insurance programs specifically for children.

Health insurance plans come in two main types: *traditional plans* and *managed care plans*. Traditional plans are *fee-for-service* plans. This means that you do not have to get approval from your insurance company before seeing a specialist. These plans are almost always more expensive than managed care plans. Managed care plans are less expensive than traditional plans but are more restrictive about which doctors you can see and which procedures will be covered under the plan.

When comparing plans, make sure you take a look at each plan's mental health benefits. If you choose to file with your insurance company for counseling visits or ADD medication visits, it is important to have a plan with good mental health benefits. Some plans have a limit on the number of visits per year, and others will only pay up to a certain dollar amount for mental health treatment. For more information on finding a medical insurance plan for you, see the Resources section at the end of this book.

HEALTH INSURANCE AND YOUR PRIVACY

If you have ever filed a claim with your medical insurance company, including for a counseling visit or medication visit for your ADD, that information is sent to a national clearinghouse called the Medical Information Bureau (MIB). When you sign a form allowing your insurance to be billed for a doctor's visit, you are also allowing MIB to collect that information. Any claim you file, whether it is for a physical ailment or for a counseling visit, is sent to MIB. This information includes the date of your visit, your diagnosis, and the medical procedure performed. This information, including a diagnosis of ADD and treatment for it, can prevent you from obtaining medical insurance, disability insurance, or life insurance in the future (Sarkis 2004). Any diagnosis on a claim you have filed can be considered a preexisting condition and may not be covered under a new insurance policy.

It is recommended that you review your record with MIB to ensure that all of the information is correct. If you do not want information about your medical treatment disclosed to the MIB, you have the option of paying for your doctor visit with your own money and not filing an insurance claim. For MIB contact information, see "Insurance Claims Clearinghouse" in the Resources section at the end of this book.

47

Catastrophic Medical Insurance

Catastrophic medical insurance only pays benefits if you need very expensive treatment. The catastrophic insurance *deductible* (money you need to pay out of pocket before your insurance starts picking up the tab) usually starts at around $5,000 (and sometimes higher). This means you will pay, out of pocket, for all of your medical expenses up to $5,000. This includes having to pay for any annual physicals, tests, and emergency room visits that your regular medical insurance doesn't cover. Catastrophic medical insurance is usually the least expensive insurance you can buy.

Life Insurance

When you have life insurance, you make the small, usually periodic payments (known as premiums) in exchange for a much larger payment from the company when you die. The money from your life insurance goes to your estate or to someone you name, known as a *beneficiary*. It is recommended that you have life insurance if family members depend on you to support them. Life insurance makes it possible for your dependents to live comfortably after your death. Because there is a higher rate of accidental death in adults with ADD, you may be even more likely to benefit from a life insurance policy than the general population (Barkley, Murphy, and Fischer 2008). There are two main kinds of life insurance: term and whole life.

TERM LIFE INSURANCE

Term life insurance only pays benefits to your beneficiary if you die within a certain time frame. For example, you can buy term life insurance that covers you for only one year. It is very inexpensive compared to whole life insurance, especially if you are young and in good health, because it is very unlikely that you will die within the time frame listed on your policy.

WHOLE LIFE INSURANCE

Whole life insurance pays benefits to your beneficiary regardless of when you die, unlike term life insurance. The insurance company takes your premiums and invests them for you to raise the cash needed to pay the promised amount on your policy. You will have to make these premium payments for many years, usually decades.

ACTIVITY: Should You Get Life Insurance?

To determine your need for life insurance, answer the following questions:

1. Do you have any children?

2. Do you have more than one child?

3. Does your spouse or partner rely on your income?

4. Do you have only a little money saved up?

5. Do you and your spouse or partner have a substantial amount of debt?

6. Does anyone in your family require full-time or special care?

If you answered yes to one or more of these questions, you should look into getting life insurance. The more children you have, the higher your income, and the more debt you have, the more likely it is that you will need life insurance. See the Resources section at the end of this book for information on determining how much life insurance you will need.

Disability Insurance

With disability insurance, you receive a portion of your current salary (usually 60 percent) or you receive a set amount of payout if you become disabled and can no longer work at your profession. Disability insurance policies differ on the total amount of benefits you can receive, when you can start receiving payments, and the duration of the payments. If you are young, you are more likely to become disabled than die. Because of this, it is probably more important for you to have disability insurance than life insurance. Also keep in mind that people with ADD have more accidents than people without ADD, at a rate of 38 percent versus 18 percent (Swensen et al. 2004). This makes it even more important for you to have disability insurance.

ACTIVITY: Find the Best Disability Insurance Policy for You

When researching different disability insurance policies, write the following information for each policy in your notebook. Use a separate page for each policy, and label that page with the name of the insurance company.

- What is the policy's definition of "disabled"? Will the policy pay benefits if you can't do your specific job, or will it only pay benefits if you can't do any job at all?

- What is the policy's *elimination period*? This is the amount of time between when you get disabled and when the policy begins to pay out to you.

- How long will the policy pay out to you in the event you become disabled? This is called the policy's *benefit period.*

- What is the maximum amount the policy will pay out to you in benefits?

- Is the insurance company fairly stable? Has it been in the news for any issues or problems?

- Are your premiums and benefits going to stay the same the entire time you have the policy, or can the insurance company change them? Look for a disability insurance policy that states that the policy is *noncancelable and guaranteed renewable.* This means that the insurance company's premiums and benefits stay the same through the duration of your policy.

Look at this information for each policy you are researching. It will make it easier for you to compare policies and make a decision. If you have any questions, contact the policy administrator. For more information on disability insurance, see the Resources section at the end of this book.

ACTIVITY: Keep Track of Your Insurance

If you have ADD, it can be difficult keeping track of any paperwork, much less a bunch of insurance policies that are difficult to understand. Copy the following list into your notebook and then fill in the information, using one notebook page per policy, so that you can better keep track of what you have; you may also discover what you still need to get to protect yourself. Having all of this information in one place can also help your family members in the event of an emergency.

- Name of insurance company

- Type (medical, catastrophic, life, disability)

- Policy number

- Premiums (per month, per year, biannually)

- Amount of coverage

- Insurance company contact information

RETIREMENT AND ADD

Like most people, you will probably retire in your early sixties. If you'd rather not retire, that is perfectly normal for people with ADD. A slowdown in the schedule does not always make for a happy ADD person. But even if you don't retire in your sixties, you will still need to put away some money for future use.

If and when you do retire, know that experiencing depression can be fairly common for people who have retired, especially if their jobs have been a large part of their identity. People with ADD are already prone to depression, and the relative lack of structure after retirement can fuel those feelings of helplessness. Make sure you stay active in your community, particularly through volunteering.

You may find you don't want to retire at all—and that is fine too. Just make sure you take enough time to enjoy nonwork-related things in life, like travel. Even if you don't have a lot of money saved up, you can still find enjoyable and fulfilling activities.

Ideas for free and low-cost activities include:

- Attending local government venues and events (parks, museums, library, art fairs, food fairs, etc.)

- Participating in community organization events (clubs or groups with public events, and religious events)

- Renting movies and/or using online DVD rental services

- Making use of senior discounts and other promotions

- Volunteering for a cause you care about (With the slowing economy, charities are hurting and they need volunteers more than ever. People with ADD are entrepreneurial and visionary; these characteristics can be of great benefit to a charity.)

If You are Already Close to (or at) Retirement

Let's say you are quickly approaching retirement or are there already and are freaking out because you don't think you've saved up enough money. You have a couple of options: continue working and/or try cutting back on some of your expenses. See chapter 6 on how to create a budget.

The Importance of Saving Up

It is important to save as much as possible as early as possible. The sooner you start saving, the more that money will grow over time. Simply put, the more money you start with or can add every now and then, the more impact you see as time goes on. Suppose you invest $100 at 10 percent interest. After one year you will have $100 plus $10 ($110). After two years you will have $110 plus $11 ($121). You make interest on the principal plus past interest payments. This is called *compound interest*. While $10 may seem trivial in this example, if you go out several years or save additional money, it can really add up.

For example, if you put $5,000 in the bank at 3 percent interest, after twenty years you will have $9,000. That's an increase of $4,000 thanks to compound interest. But what if you start with $5,000 and then add $100 to that account each month for twenty years? You would have contributed $5,000 + $24,000 = $29,000, but thanks to the interest on your additional savings, you would have $42,000, an increase of $13,000!

WILLS

A *will* is a legal document that states what should happen to your personal belongings and money after your death. It is always in your best interest to have a will. When you don't have a will, the court gets to decide how to distribute assets from your estate. This is different than a *living will*, which is a document that states your decisions about being on life support and the use of heroic measures in the event you are physically incapacitated.

The more detail you put into your documents and will, the better. When there is a death in the family, it can change relationships quickly. People can act in unexpected ways when they are in shock and grieving. Instead of saying, "My jewelry should be divided between my two children," write specifically which pieces go to whom. This creates a more efficient method of dividing the assets and results in less disagreement among family members. When you are writing your will, you can name a charity to which you would like to leave part (or all) of your assets. You may even think you don't have any assets, but you still have items that you may want to leave to certain people.

A will specifies the name of an executor (or executors). The *executor* is the person put in charge of carrying out the specifics of a will. You may want to consider appointing an attorney instead of a family member as the executor of your estate. This reduces the chances of conflict among family members.

Use an Attorney or Do It Yourself?

If you are concerned about the cost of an attorney when creating a will, consider this: if you have considerable assets or own your own business, not consulting an attorney may cost you and your family a lot more money in the long run.

There are also software programs and do-it-yourself books available for creating wills. This may be a viable option if you meet the following criteria:

- You have a relatively small amount of assets.
- You have only one adult child.
- You are legally married to your partner.
- All of the real estate property (houses or condominiums) you own is in the same state you live in.
- You want to give your assets to your spouse or child(ren).

If you have any questions about which route you should take when creating a will, consult an attorney who has experience in estate law.

Estate Taxes and Gift Tax

In the United States, *estate taxes* are levied on the assets remaining after a person's death. Attorneys know how to set up your will so that you can pay the least amount of estate tax possible. Why donate money to the government when you don't need to?

You may be thinking that to avoid estate taxes, you will have to start giving away all of your money now. Before you do that, be aware that there is something called a *gift tax*. This means that if you give more than $11,000 to a person in one year, you (the giver) must pay a tax on that money. Exclusions to this include paying for someone's tuition or medical expenses, gifts to your spouse, and contributions to a political organization.

See an accountant or attorney to determine the best way to organize your estate. For more information on estate taxes and gift taxes, see the Resources section at the end of this book.

ACTIVITY: Setting Up a Will

Before you go to an attorney or do a will yourself, it is helpful to have an idea of what items you want to leave to others and to what charities, if any, you would like to leave money. Divide one of your notebook pages into two columns—one column labeled "Item" and the other column labeled "Give to" for the name of the person to whom you would like to give the item. Fill in this information to give yourself a jump start on your will. Remember to include artwork, jewelry, or any items with sentimental value. Leave yourself some space at the bottom of the page to create a list labeled "Charities I would like to include in my will."

When you are ready to create your will, take your notebook to your attorney's office to further ensure that your requests will be fulfilled.

SUMMARY

In this chapter, you learned how to prepare financially for your and your family's future by putting the maximum amount in your retirement accounts, protecting yourself with insurance, and having a will. In the next chapter, you will learn how to invest your hard-earned money.

CHAPTER 4

Investing

Because of their difficulties with executive functions, people with ADD find it challenging to plan ahead for the long term and to see the consequences of their actions. As you read in chapter 3, many people with ADD have not set up the investment accounts that might provide them with money to live on when they retire.

In this chapter, you will learn about three different ways to invest money—in stocks, mutual funds, and bonds. You will also learn how to go about buying and selling your investments, and you will find out which financial professionals can best help you.

WHAT DOES "INVESTING" MEAN?

Investing means putting money into a financial product or plan so you can get a *return* (profit). Because people with ADD usually operate in the "here and now," you may not be able to visualize getting $1,500 in a few years from the $1,000 you invest now. Why not just spend that money now on something you really want? However, you should be investing your money so that you are earning money without really having to work for it—what a bonus! And the sooner you put money away in an investment, the less likely you are to spend it impulsively.

TYPES OF INVESTMENTS

The three most popular types of investments are stocks, bonds, and mutual funds. Each has its own benefits and drawbacks. You will now learn about each of these investments and will get a better idea of which ones might be best for you.

Stocks

When you buy *stock* in a company, it means you own a part of the company. You are now an investor in that company, no matter how little or how much stock you own. When one person, or a group of people together, hold a majority of the stock in a corporation, they usually control it. This means they have the right to make decisions about the company's actions.

Stocks are important investments because they usually increase in value over time more than other types of investments. If they do increase in value, you can sell them for more than you paid for them, thus making a profit. However, stocks sometimes lose value, and if you sell a stock for less than you paid for it, you lose money. Stocks are riskier than mutual funds and bonds, but the potential for profit is greater.

STOCK SPLITS

When the price of a stock increases, a company may have what is called a *stock split,* whereby the number of shares doubles but the price is halved. For example, if a company announces it is having a two-for-one stock split, this means that for every share of stock you have, you will now have two shares. However, the price of each share is cut in half. This makes it is easier for other people to buy shares, since the shares are now at a lower price. So if you own one hundred shares of this stock and shares are selling for $100 each, a two-for-one stock split means that you now have two hundred shares that are each worth $50. Stock splits might not hurt or help you directly, but the new per-share price may attract more buyers, thus increasing the stock price if the company is a good investment choice. In that case, stock splits are a good thing because each of your now two hundred shares might go up in value as new investors buy shares. If the price went back to $100, you would then have a $20,000 investment—a $10,000 increase from before the stock split.

DIVIDENDS

A *dividend* is money that a company pays out to its stockholders. Some companies pay out dividends on a regular basis, but they are not obligated to do so if their profits fall. When you get a dividend distribution, you can tell your investment professional to reinvest the shares, you can keep the money in cash reserves in your account (if you want to buy other stocks), or you can receive it as cash. The option you choose depends on your financial standing in life. If you are retired and are living on a fixed income, you may want to use the dividends as extra income, while if you are young and relatively debt free, you may want to reinvest the money by buying more stock.

A CAUTION ABOUT DAY-TRADING

Day traders buy and sell stocks rapidly throughout the course of a day via the Internet. Some consider this to be a form of gambling. While it was more widespread in the late 1990s, it still exists today. People with ADD are especially susceptible to getting caught up in day-trading due to its fast-paced nature and the high that people with ADD often get from creating "crisis" conditions.

Unfortunately, day-trading has a downside—addiction and a rapid loss of money. Along with the extreme highs of day-trading come extreme lows. Since most people who try day-trading lose money, the safest policy is to buy your stocks, hold on to them until you are ready to sell them, and avoid day-trading altogether.

Bonds

Bonds are the debts of governments, utilities, and large corporations. For example, if a county government needs money for its school system, it can borrow money from investors in the form of bonds. Typically, bonds pay a specific amount of interest until a certain date. On that date, the principal of the bond is repaid to the investor. Bonds are seen as being safer investments than stocks because bond payments are usually guaranteed. If you are a first-time investor, it is recommended that you focus on stocks and mutual funds instead of bonds because of the intricacies involved, which include complicating your taxes.

Mutual Funds

Most *mutual funds* are investments that consist of stocks and bonds from different companies. Often the companies in a mutual fund have something in common—for example, they may all be small businesses or based in a foreign country. You buy shares in a mutual fund just like you buy individual stock. There are many, many mutual funds for you to choose from. There is a cost to operating a mutual fund (hiring staff, renting an office, etc.), so mutual funds charge some money to own shares, either in the form of a *load* or an *expense ratio*.

MUTUAL FUND LOADS

Some mutual funds will charge a fee either when you buy in to the fund or when you sell it. If you are charged when you buy in to a fund, it is called a *front-end load*. If you are charged when you sell, it is called a *back-end load*. Funds that do not charge a load are called *no-load funds*.

MUTUAL FUND EXPENSE RATIOS

The *expense ratio* is usually given as a percentage of the fund size. For example, an expense ratio of 1 percent for a $100 million fund means that it costs $1 million a year to pay the salaries of the manager (or management team) and for the office lease, marketing materials, and so on. These costs are passed on to you in the form of reduced distributions and/or lower share values. You might think a fund with a higher expense ratio will perform better, but that is not necessarily true. For help in determining which fund is best for you, see the Resources section at the end of this book.

FIGURE OUT YOUR BEST INVESTMENT STRATEGY

The amount of money you put into investing and the level of risk you want to take depends on where you are in life. If you are young and building up your financial portfolio, you may be more willing to invest in stocks or mutual funds that are more likely to fluctuate in value. This is known as investing *aggressively*. Aggressive investments include many information technology and biotechnology stocks.

If you are retired and living off your savings, you may want to be more conservative with your investments. You may want to choose stocks and mutual funds that are steady and aren't as likely to fluctuate in price. These are called *conservative* investments. These investments include purchasing stock in a utility company. The more time you have ahead of you to invest, the more likely you are to want to choose investments wherein you can accrue more money and will have more time to bounce back if an investment's price drops.

Regardless of your age or financial standing in life, it is always good to *diversify* your portfolio. This means that if you are an aggressive investor, you will want a majority of your investments to be of higher risk but you should be sure to invest a certain percentage in less risky investments. If you are a more conservative investor, you will want a majority of your investments to be in the low-risk category but a small percentage in possibly riskier investments. Your investment professional can help you determine the best balance for your portfolio. You can also find online resources in the Resources section (under "Financial Risk Quiz") at the end of this book. To determine your appropriate level of risk, complete the activity below.

ACTIVITY: Determine Your Level of Financial Risk

Take the following quiz to determine if you should focus more on aggressive investments or on conservative investments.

1. I am close to retirement.

   a. No

   b. Yes

2. If my stock dropped in value suddenly, my first reaction would be

   a. A little concern

   b. Panic

3. When I retire, I will be relying

   a. On additional sources of income

   b. Solely on my investment accounts

4. I would rather have

   a. A high rate of return on my investments

   b. A lower rate of return if it means my investments don't fluctuate wildly in value

5. I will need to use the money in my investment account

   a. Twenty years from now, at the earliest

   b. Within the next few years

If you answered mostly A's, you tend to fit the profile of an aggressive investor. If you answered mostly B's, you may want to be more conservative with your investments and stick with slower-growth stocks. For suggestions on how to diversify your portfolio for each type, read below. See your investment professional if you have any questions about how to use your risk profile to your best advantage.

Portfolios for the Aggressive or Conservative Investor

Now that you have completed the activity above and determined whether you are an aggressive or conservative investor, here are some suggestions for how you should divide your portfolio.

If you are willing to take on more risk, your portfolio will be more aggressive, which means you will have most of your money in *equities* (stocks) and only a small part in bonds or similar fixed-income securities. For example, a moderately aggressive portfolio is about 50 percent stocks, 35 percent bonds, and 15 percent cash or cash equivalents (such as certificates of deposit [CDs] or short-term treasury certificates). If you want to take on less risk, you would look for a conservative portfolio that holds mostly fixed-income securities. An example of a conservative portfolio would be 75 percent bonds, 15 percent stocks, and 10 percent cash.

Remember, if you have an aggressive portfolio, you could make a lot more money than if you have a conservative one, but you could also lose a lot more money. If you are not comfortable with investing, or cannot stand the thought of losing money, you should seriously consider having a more conservative portfolio.

Deciding to Invest or Pay Off Debt

You may have come upon an unexpected amount of money or you may have received a bonus. You may be wondering if it is wiser to invest the money or to use it to pay off your credit cards, car loan, student loan, or other debt. Due to interest rates, the amount of money you will owe on your debt will most likely increase more than the money you will earn on any investments. For that reason, you may want to consider paying off your debts before investing the money. For example, a credit card that has an 11 percent interest rate is charging you a higher interest rate on your debt than you would earn from an investment. If you choose to pay off debt, it is recommended that you begin with the debt that has the highest interest rate first. You will learn more about paying off your debts in chapter 8.

CHECKING ON YOUR INVESTMENTS

It can be easy to fall into the trap of continually checking your investments online, even to the point where you are checking on them up to several times a day. It isn't necessary to continually check, and doing so can cause you undue stress. Continually checking your investments creates a feeling of panic, which can cause you to make even more impulsive decisions. If you must check your investments daily, just check them at the beginning and the end of the day.

I Need to Sell My Stock Now!

One of the things about obsessively checking your investments is that it tempts you to want to sell them as soon as things start heading south. Remember that most everything in life is cyclical—what goes up must come down and vice versa. Before you sell your stock, sit on the idea for a day. If you impulsively sell, you may find that the stock you sold yesterday makes big gains today—but if you've sold it, you'll have missed out.

ACTIVITY: Is It Time to Sell My Stock?

You may want to sell your stocks as soon as they start dropping in value, but before you do that, see if you can answer yes to one or more of the following questions:

1. Am I having a moral or ethical issue with the company?

2. Do I have debts at high interest rates and could I use the cash to pay those debts?

3. Is this stock much riskier than I thought it would be? Does the price fluctuate too wildly for my taste?

4. In researching the company, have I found that its business has declined and may affect the value of the stock?

5. Have I found another company in the same industry whose stock might perform better than this stock?

6. Does the stock price continue to fall for weeks or months with no publicly given reason as to why?

7. Have I met with my investment professional who agrees this would be a good time to sell the stock and can provide good reasons for doing so?

The more of these questions you can answer yes to, the more of a valid case you have for selling your stock.

HOW TO RESEARCH YOUR INVESTMENTS

It is recommended that you buy the stock of a company with which you are familiar, one whose products or services you have used. Someone, such as an investment professional, might recommend a particular stock to you. Even if you have a recommendation, research the company yourself by looking at its annual report online or by looking for it on financial websites. When you look at a company's annual report, look over the auditor's report and financial statements. In addition, look at the section titled "Management's Discussion and Analysis" (MD&A). The information you are looking for in the MD&A is the company's statement about the risks and downsides it faces. If it doesn't look good, don't worry. The MD&A is required to list all foreseeable risks to the company, and you may see things you had not considered. It discusses the company's financial issues, compliance with laws and regulations, and also includes how the company plans to fix any problems. Decide for yourself if these risks are something you are comfortable with; if so, you will be investing with a better understanding of the company and its operating challenges.

When looking at financial websites, look for recent articles or press releases about the company. Keep in mind that you can still invest even if you don't do this type of research. But research is a very helpful tool for making wise investment choices. See "Investment Research" in the Resources section at the end of this book for recommended websites for research.

ACTIVITY: Find and Research Your Favorite Companies

What products or services do you personally use that you feel are really outstanding? Is there a national restaurant chain you love to visit or a store in the mall you feel has great customer service and prices? It pays to invest in what *you* know firsthand as a consumer. Make a list in your notebook of two or three businesses in each of the following categories that you personally think very highly of and enjoy using:

- Clothing brands

- Fast-food chains and restaurants

- Retail stores

- Gas stations

- Entertainment

- Home or beauty products

Then ask yourself if you think you, and other people, will use less, the same amount, or more of those products in the next few years. If the answer is "the same or more," then do more research on those companies and consider adding them to your portfolio!

KEEP A RECORD OF YOUR INVESTMENTS

It is important to be aware of what you own, especially if you and/or your spouse invest through different brokerages. This may be the case if you and your spouse work at different companies and have different retirement or investment plans. You will learn more about keeping your financial documents organized in chapter 5.

BUYING AND SELLING YOUR INVESTMENTS

To buy or sell your investments, whether they are stocks, bonds, or mutual funds, you can either meet with your investment professional in person or you can do trading over the Internet. If you have ADD, it may be best to meet with your investment professional in person so there is less chance that you will make impulsive decisions. If you have just started investing and you are not yet working with an investment professional, continue reading so you can learn how to pick the best person for you.

Using an Investment Professional

If you are a first-time investor, we recommended that you use the services of a personal investment advisor. You can also buy and sell investment products yourself using an online brokerage firm. Most online brokers have investment advisers on staff whom you can call for general advice. An investment professional takes time to learn about your financial goals and risk fears. You can find advisory firms both nationwide and locally. It's usually good to get a recommendation from a family member or friend.

Any investment professional who advises people on buying stocks, bonds, or mutual funds has passed certain examinations and background checks to be licensed by the Financial Industry Regulatory Authority (FINRA), formerly the National Association of Security Dealers (NASD). Additionally, a good investment professional usually has a college degree in business (BA or MBA) or a specialized certification, such as a Chartered Financial Analyst (CFA) certification. Remember, just because someone claims to be an investment professional or has one of these certifications, it does not mean you should just give your money to him or her to invest or should blindly follow his or her advice. The professional must take the time to know what your financial goals are and what level of risk you are willing to accept. For help on determining which level of financial risk you should be willing to take, see the Resources section at the end of this book.

SUMMARY

In this chapter, you learned about the different types of investments, tips for checking and researching your investments, and the types of investment professionals available to help you. In the next chapter, you will learn how to organize all your investment statements and other important financial documents.

CHAPTER 5

Organizing Your Money

In chapter 4, you learned about investing in stocks, bonds, and mutual funds. There are a lot of documents that go along with those investments. In this chapter, you will learn how to keep all of your financial documents organized and accessible.

ADD AND ORGANIZATION

Money management involves both organizational skills and the ability to do tedious detail work. No wonder people with ADD have difficulties managing their money! It is normal to feel overwhelmed and to have even more difficulty focusing than usual when you try to organize your money. This is why it is so important that you have an ADD-friendly financial organization system. You need a system that is simple and easy to maintain.

Thanks to computer technology, there is less and less of a need to have paper versions of data that you can access on your computer or online. The less paper you have, the less clutter you have. In this chapter, you will learn how to go paperless if possible and when to keep a paper copy.

MONEY MANAGEMENT SOFTWARE

Why try to keep track of all the details about managing your money yourself when you can use software? Money management software can help you by performing the following tasks:

- Balancing your checkbook

- Organizing your investments and updating their value daily

- Reminding you when bills are due

- Paying your bills over the Internet

- Providing graphs of your spending and saving habits

- Printing out a list of your tax-deductible expenses

- Filing your taxes online

If you have a bank with online banking services, or your investment service has online updates, you can have this information automatically downloaded to your money management software.

You will be much more successful at using the software if you take a class on how to use it, know someone who can tutor you, or better, hire an assistant to do it for you. You can learn more about hiring an assistant later in this chapter.

Money management software takes away a lot of the monotony and detail of money management. Once you have gotten into the habit of using the software, you will be able to keep more money in the bank. You will no longer be losing money because of late fees or bounced checks. You will also have less stress, since the computer reminds you to pay your bills. You may even realize that you have more money than you thought and wind up with more money than you ever imagined! See the Resources section at the end of this book for more information on money management software.

ACTIVITY: What Money Organization Techniques Have Worked or Not Worked in the Past?

To figure out the best money organization system for you, it is important to review what has or has not worked for you in the past. Many well-meaning family members, friends, and even books on organizing can help you set up an organization system, but it might be complicated for someone with ADD. The more complicated the system, the harder it is to keep up. Remember, simplicity is best. What methods have you used in the past to organize your financial documents?

Get your notebook and pen. You will be using this notebook to complete the activities throughout this chapter. First, write down the organizational issue that concerns you. Next, write down what method or item you used to get this situation in order or under control. Then write down whether this method worked for you or did not work, and why. Finally, write a possible alternative solution to the issue. Here's an example:

Issue: My receipts were all over the place, and I could not locate them at tax time.

Method or item used: I kept all of my receipts in one folder.

Outcome: This did *not* work for me because when it came time to do my taxes, I had to sort out all the current receipts from the pile.

Possible solution: I can keep my receipts together by year. This will make them easier to put together at tax time.

Balancing Your Checkbook

You may never have balanced a checkbook—you may not even know what that means. *Balancing a checkbook* means you keep track of which checks have been deposited by your payees. You also keep track of withdrawals you have made with your debit card and through automatic withdrawal (both of which you will learn more about in chapter 9). When you balance your checkbook, you are making sure your account balance is the same as the balance on your bank statement.

If you have a math learning disability, as many people with ADD do, it can be difficult for you to add and subtract. You may also have difficulty keeping the digits in the correct columns when you add or subtract, resulting in some very interesting arithmetic. This is why using money management software is essential for a person with ADD. You can click a button, and the software automatically balances your checkbook and can tell you if a check is still outstanding (and not in the sense that it is fabulous and a high achiever!) An *outstanding* check is one that someone has not deposited, meaning you need to make sure you have enough money in the bank to cover the amount of this check.

Money management software can also show you where your money is going. You can figure out how much money is going toward your health care, dining out, clothing, and a wide variety of other categories. This information is displayed in a graph. Graphs may be particularly helpful for you because, like many people with ADD, you may have an easier time processing information in a visual format.

KEEP YOUR BILLS ORGANIZED

You may have experienced either losing a bill or just forgetting to pay it—this is very common for people with ADD. This can lead to late fees and can even hurt your credit. To prevent this from happening, it is best to keep all of your bills in one place. Fill a basket with some envelopes, stamps, your checkbook, and a pen. When a bill comes in the mail, bring it to the bill-paying basket and write a check right then and there. You can call companies and ask them to reschedule your bill due dates so they all fall on the same day, or you can schedule your bill due dates in two batches, which may be preferable if you receive two paychecks a month.

An even easier and more efficient option is to sign up for electronic withdrawal. This way your bills are paid automatically, and you don't even have to worry about mailing off a check on time. You just have to make sure you have enough money in your account each month to cover these bills. You should check your statements regularly to make sure the proper amount is being automatically withdrawn. You should also check to make sure that a company providing a service that you canceled isn't continuing to make withdrawals out of your account.

ACTIVITY: Keep Track of Automatic Withdrawals

There are a variety of services that allow you to use automatic withdrawal. In your notebook, write down the names of these services. Then put a check next to the ones you pay with automatic withdrawal. Next write the date of withdrawal for each service. If you have more than one checking account, it is important to write down which account is being used for each automatic withdrawal. Here is a list to get you started:

- Cable

- Internet

- Electricity

- Water/sewer

- Credit card 1

- Credit card 2

- Student loan payment

- Car loan payment

- Mortgage payment

- Rent payment

By keeping track of each of these withdrawals, you will be less likely to have an overdrawn account. You can use the list you have made to make sure you have the correct amounts recorded in your online money management software or checkbook. Be on the lookout for other monthly payments that you could make with automatic withdrawals.

STORING FINANCIAL DOCUMENTS

Trying to store important papers efficiently and neatly can be the bane of an ADD person's existence. You will now learn a relatively simple way to file your financial papers (and other important papers) in order to keep them organized.

Use File Folders

Use hanging file folders to hold documents. These are large folders in which you can keep several smaller file folders. Each hanging file folder should have the name of a particular category of your finances. Here are possible categories you can use:

- Auto

- Credit Cards

- Insurance

- Investments

- Home

- Loans

- Warranties

Each hanging file folder then contains file folders that fit each category. For example, the "Auto" folder can contain file folders for your car title or car loan paperwork. In the hanging folder labeled "Home," you can have file folders labeled for your mortgage papers, your home equity loan papers, and a copy of the deed on your home. We recommend that you purchase colored file folders instead of the plain manila ones. People with ADD are much more likely to keep things organized and be able to find things if they are color-coded. For example, if you have a red car, use a red "Auto" hanging file and make all the file folders inside it red as well.

The best place to keep files is in a metal, lockable file cabinet. If you can't have a file cabinet because of space constraints, a good solution is to organize your folders in a plastic storage bin from an office supply store (the kind with translucent plastic walls and a hinged lid to keep dust and liquids out; these also stack for archiving).

Use a Label Maker

Because many people with ADD have difficulty with legible handwriting, it is very helpful and much more efficient to use a label machine. You type in what you want on the label, and it prints it right out. This way you can immediately see what is in a file cabinet or other storage container. Labelers can be purchased at any office supply store. For more information, see the Resources section at the end of this book.

KEEPING AND STORING RECEIPTS

Receipts are little pieces of paper that can get totally out of control and take up valuable counter space. It may even feel like the receipts multiply on their own! Receipts combine two of the most challenging things for people with ADD—they contain detailed and sometimes important information and they are small enough to get easily lost.

What Receipts Do You Really Need to Keep?

To reduce clutter, it is best to keep only the receipts you need. You may be looking at the pile of receipts on your desk (or the loose ones scattered throughout your home) and wondering how you will sift through all of them. Some of those receipts will be useful to you, and some can be tossed out.

Keep any receipts, credit card statements, or bank statements related to business expenses, because these expenses are *tax deductible*. This means that the amounts of these expenses are subtracted from the revenues of the business. If you pay cash for a business expense and then lose that receipt, you may lose that deduction from your taxes. If you use a credit card when you make business purchases, use one particular credit card. This will make it much simpler for you to retrieve the details on your business purchases around tax time. Keep receipts for medical expenses, as these may also be tax deductible. Also keep receipts for important purchases, especially if there is also a warranty with the item. If you have mailed in a copy of a receipt for a rebate, keep the original until you receive your rebate check.

The Internal Revenue Service (IRS) does not require a receipt for anything under $75. Some financial professionals may recommend that you keep these receipts anyway. However, if you have ADD and are prone to clutter, it may be better to toss these receipts after you have recorded the amount for your taxes.

Use a Receipt Scanner

A receipt scanner can help you keep track of your receipts and cut down on the clutter. At tax time, you can search through your scanned receipts by category to find your tax-deductible items. This is especially helpful if you have paid for an item with cash, as those paper receipts can be easy to lose track of at tax time. By using a receipt scanner, you now have all your cash receipts in one spot.

Once you scan the receipt, and you verify that the scanned copy is readable, you can throw out the receipt. The IRS accepts electronic scans of receipts for tax purposes. You might find that scanning your receipts is more of a time-eater than a time-saver. It's entirely up to you to decide if the time investment is worth it. See the Resources section at the end of this book for more information on receipt scanners.

THERMAL RECEIPTS

Some receipts are printed on thermal paper—a type of paper that feels almost slick to the touch. These receipts can fade quickly, so it is important to scan your important thermal receipts first above all others. If you don't have a scanner, at least make a photocopy of thermal receipts.

BACK UP YOUR COMPUTER'S HARD DRIVE

If you are storing any financial documents on your computer and do not have a paper version, be sure you back up your hard drive regularly so that you have more than one electronic copy of all your money management software and scanned-receipt data.

External Hard Drives

You can buy an external hard drive for your computer and schedule it to automatically back up all of your files. While you might think an external hard drive is pricey, it is much more costly to lose your financial information (and other data) if your computer crashes. Make sure the data on your hard drive is encrypted (an added layer of security). Store your hard drive in a secure location, such as a locked cabinet or small safe at home. You can also store your hard drive in a safe deposit box.

Online Backup

There are services available that will store your hard drive information online for a low monthly fee. You may even be able to get the service for free on some sites if your backup is less than one gigabyte. This may be enough space for your financial records. An advantage to having your data backed up online is that if your computer and external hard drive are damaged, you still have access to your information. Make sure the site is reputable, has been in business for a while, and that the storage is encrypted. For more information on online backup services, see the Resources section at the end of this book.

GET OUTSIDE HELP KEEPING YOUR MONEY ORGANIZED

Realizing you need help getting your financial documents organized isn't a sign of weakness—it is a sign of strength and an acknowledgment that no one can do everything on his or her own.

Hire Someone to Do Your Taxes

Your expertise is not in organizing and analyzing little bits of information—so why wear yourself out trying to do it? Put your time and energy into things you enjoy and are good at. You can hire someone to do your taxes for a reasonable fee. It does help, however, to have your receipts and other necessary tax items organized in some way before you show up to get your taxes done. The benefits of having someone do your taxes outweigh the costs. A tax expert will ask you questions that can wind up saving you a lot of money. Tax software is also available, but if you have ADD, you may find that meeting with someone in person is better for keeping you focused.

Hire an Assistant

You may feel that you can't afford to pay an assistant to organize your finances, but think of the money you will save once you are paying your bills on time, and the time and energy you will save because you know where all your receipts are at tax time!

You can hire an assistant either through an ad or by asking for a referral from your family and friends. You can also ask a trusted family member or friend to help you out, but make sure it is someone who will keep your financial information confidential.

Keep in mind that you are allowing this person access to your financial information, so make sure you conduct a background check. A background check can be done by contacting your local and state law enforcement agencies. You can also do a background check through an online service. For more information on background check services, see the Resources section at the end of this book. If your intuition tells you to be cautious about hiring someone, listen to it!

It is up to you to decide how many hours a week you need your assistant. Some people find that it works best to have the assistant come in more frequently at the beginning of the process, while the papers are being organized, and less frequently once order has been established and needs only to be maintained.

ACTIVITY: Hiring an Assistant

When interviewing a potential assistant, write down his or her answers to the following questions in your notebook:

- What is your previous experience with managing finances?

- Do you have training with money management software?

- What days and hours are you available?

- Why did you leave your last job?

- Have you previously worked with people who have issues with chronic disorganization?

- How will you cope if something that you organized has become disorganized again by your next visit?

Getting the answers to these questions will help you determine if your interviewee is a good fit. And by writing down the answers in your notebook, you can share that information later with a spouse or partner who wasn't able to attend the interview.

TASKS FOR YOUR FINANCIAL ASSISTANT

Your assistant can help with a wide variety of tasks, including the following:

- Setting up money management software

- Entering checks into money management software

- Determining if receipts need to be kept or tossed

- Writing checks out for you (you would still need to sign them)

- Keeping track of bills

- Setting up automatic withdrawal and deposit

- Creating categories and writing labels for file folders

- Filing documents

- Labeling folders and storage containers

You can also ask your assistant for recommendations for any other ways you can organize your finances. Remember to keep an open mind, but also let your assistant know if you think a particular method of organization might be a challenge for you. Keeping finances organized is an ongoing process, but if your assistant has some extra time, see if he or she can help you organize other areas of the house.

It is helpful if you and your partner let your assistant know how you would like to be redirected if he or she feels you are not focusing on the task at hand. You can ask your assistant to say your name or to ask you to make eye contact if he or she notices you are distracted. You can even make up a code word that will remind you to stay on task. It all depends on what is comfortable for and helpful to both you and your assistant. You can also let your assistant know how long you can work on a task before you get distracted. For some people, the time limit is thirty minutes—for others, one hour. Your assistant can keep track of time and let you know when it is time to take a break.

HOW LONG SHOULD YOU KEEP FINANCIAL DOCUMENTS?

There are different recommended time frames for disposing of your financial papers, depending on the type of document.

- Bank statements and canceled checks—Keep them for seven years.

- Tax records—The guideline is seven years, but keeping your tax returns indefinitely is ideal.

- Automatic teller machine (ATM) slips—Match them with your bank statement and then throw them away.

- Receipts for everyday items—Check them against your bank records and then throw them away, unless you might need to return the item.

- Receipts for important purchases—Keep them for the length of time you have the item, especially if there is a warranty involved. If you keep the instruction booklet that came with your purchase, you can staple the receipt to the front cover.

- Mortgage papers—Keep them as long as you own the home or for seven years after fulfillment of the loan.

- Credit card statements—Keep them for seven years if needed for your taxes.

- Receipts or utility bills for which you claim a tax deduction— Keep these with your tax records.

- Trade confirmations and year-end reports from banks and brokerages—Keep these with your tax records.

- Trade confirmations for stocks and any statements about dividend reinvestments—Keep until you sell all of those shares. Without statements, it might be difficult to figure out the original purchase cost of the shares when you want to sell them, especially if you bought the stock a while ago. (See chapter 4 for more information on dividends.)

ACTIVITY: Keep Track of Your Financial Documents

Keeping track of when you should throw something out and where you have stored it can really reduce the amount of clutter in your home. Using your notebook, first write at the top of the page the type of document you are storing (for example, bank statements, canceled checks, credit card statements, and other financial documents). Then write the date you stored this document. People with ADD tend to store things in a "special location," which they have difficulty remembering later! For that reason, also write the location where you stored the documents. Then, using the guidelines in the list above, write the date when you can shred that particular set of documents. Repeat this process on a separate page in the notebook for each type of document to keep everything uncluttered and easy to read.

IDENTITY THEFT AND THE IMPORTANCE OF SHREDDING

When someone uses your social security number or other identifiable information to obtain goods, services, or money as if he or she were you, this is called *identity theft*. From 2003 to 2006, the rate of identity theft increased

50 percent. During this time period, fifteen million people in the United States experienced someone stealing their identity (Soat 2007).

While ATM receipts show little identifying information, documents such as utility bills; bank, brokerage, and credit card statements; and especially tax records are highly sought after by identity theft criminals, who will use this information to pose as you to purchase items or worse, to empty out your accounts. This can lead to years of trying to untangle the chaos created in your life, not to mention damage to your credit.

While the risk of identity theft is relatively small, shredding documents is so easy that the benefits most definitely outweigh the drawbacks. When discarding your financial documents, use a cross-cut shredder. Cross-cut shredders make it even more difficult for identity thieves to piece together discarded documents. You can get a cross-cut shredder from any office supply store. (See the Resources section at the end of this book for office supply sources.) You may also be able to bring your documents to your bank, where they will shred them for no charge, but having a shredder at home is much easier and more efficient. The quicker you can get rid of unneeded paper, the better.

SUMMARY

In this chapter, you learned ways to get your financial documents organized and to keep them that way. You also learned when to keep documents, when to shred them, and when to seek outside help. In chapter 6, you will learn the joys of budgeting.

CHAPTER 6

Budgeting

A budget is a tool that helps you determine how much money you can spend each month in different areas of your life. Budgeting involves a number of things that are not an ADD person's strengths—organization, detail-oriented work, and planning ahead. However, you *can* create a budget that you can manage. In this chapter, you will discover the difference between needs and wants, how to create your own budget, and how to determine your financial goals.

Budgets are important because they can do the following:

- Keep you on track with your financial goals

- Decrease your chances of being overdrawn in your accounts

- Increase your amount of savings

- Point out where you may be paying too much or unnecessarily for items or services

Before you create your budget, you will first learn the difference between needs and wants and between fixed and flexible expenses.

NEEDS AND WANTS

There are things we need in life and things that we just want. Due to impulsivity, it can be difficult for someone with ADD to tell the difference between the two. *Needs* are those things that you must have in order to survive:

- Shelter

- Food

- Water

- Clothing

- Medical care

- Transportation

Wants are things you would like to have but that aren't necessary to your survival. They include things like:

- A large house

- Designer clothes

- Electronic gadgets

- A new car

Needs and wants may differ from person to person based on your job and your family. Here is an example of the difference between a need and want: You may say, "I need that new cell phone! It will help me be more productive and I need to look successful." You may *want* that new cell phone, but you will not die without it (even though it might feel like it). Water, food, and shelter—you definitely need those to survive.

The more you are able to manage your money, the more you will be able to buy "wants" in addition to "needs." One of the ways to be able to buy your "wants" is to create and follow a budget.

FIXED AND FLEXIBLE EXPENSES

Fixed expenses are costs that stay the same each month. They are costs that you pay periodically (monthly, yearly, etc.) and that are the same amount each time. Examples of fixed expenses are your rent or mortgage, car payment, or student loan payment. *Flexible expenses* are costs that you can spend less or more on without affecting your overall standard of living. This includes items like groceries (which can be both needs and wants) or enter-tainment. For example, spending money on going to the movies is a flexible expense. You don't *need* to go to the movies every weekend—it is not a life-or-death issue. However, with your mortgage, you can't skip paying for a month without hearing from the bank about the consequences.

Knowing the difference between your fixed and flexible expenses can help you determine realistically those areas in which you can spend less money. Fixed expenses include the following:

- Rent or mortgage

- Student loan payment

- Car payment

- Insurance premiums

Flexible expenses include the following:

- Entertainment costs

- Clothing

- Vacations

- Gifts

Medication Is a Fixed Expense

Too often, people with ADD will view medication as a flexible expense. They figure that they don't really *need* it, so they start taking their medication every other day or don't get the prescription refilled.

It is recommended that you view your medication as a fixed expense. More than likely, there are other areas where you can scale back in order to afford your medication. You can also ask your doctor about generic equivalents for brand-name medications.

Medication can actually save you money in the long run—for example, you are less likely to make errors at work, which could cost you a promotion or even your job! You are also less likely to get traffic tickets or to get into costly accidents (Matza, Paramore, and Prasad 2005). So medication is actually a money-saver in the long run.

ACTIVITY: Create a Budget

Use the following activity to determine your monthly budget. You don't need to get the amounts down to the penny. Just writing a dollar amount is fine.

Using your notebook, begin by writing down your monthly income. Because many people with ADD have difficulties with math, here are some formulas for figuring out your monthly income:

- Weekly pay times four

- Bimonthly pay times two

- If your income varies widely from month to month, find out the yearly total and divide by twelve.

Now make a list like the one below and fill in your fixed and flexible expenses in your notebook. As you read earlier in this chapter, fixed expenses are those for which you pay a set amount from month to month. Flexible expenses are those that you have some leeway in the amount you are paying. If you pay your car insurance every six months, divide that payment by six to get your monthly payment. Remember that this budget is just a guideline. Feel free to add or delete items as you see fit.

Income

Work   _____

Other income   _____

Total: _____

Fixed Expenses

Car payment   _____

Rent   _____

Cable   _____

Internet   _____

Electricity   _____

Gas   _____

Telephone   _____

Tuition   _____

Car insurance   _____

Health insurance _____

Medications   _____

Fuel (gasoline)   _____

Child support   _____

Alimony   _____

Total: _____

Flexible Expenses

Eating out   _____

Snacks   _____

Vacations/trips   _____

Concerts/music   _____

Game tickets
(This may be a fixed
expense for some.)   _____

Groceries   _____

Clothing   _____

Gifts   _____

Hobbies   _____

Total: _____

***Total of fixed plus
flexible expenses:***   _____

Income minus expenses: _____

Your main goal is to have money left over after you subtract your expenses from your income. Even if that number is just $20 or $30, you are still on the right track. In the following months, keep track of your expenses to see if your budget estimates are accurate. You may be surprised to see expenses you hadn't thought of before and you may realize you don't spend as much money in a particular category as you thought. The beauty of a budget is that you can change it as your life and your needs change.

If you find you have a negative number after subtracting your expenses from your income, the important thing is that you now know your financial standing. And you can take steps toward improving your monthly balance.

FIXING YOUR BUDGET

To create a surplus of money at the end of the month, look at categories where you can reduce your expenses. First look at your flexible expenses. Are you eating out frequently? Are you buying clothing when you have more than enough already?

If you've adjusted your flexible expenses and you still don't have any money left over at the end of the month, look at your fixed expenses. Ideas for cutting back on your fixed expenses include reducing the number of cable channels you receive and checking with your car insurance company to see if it has any special discount offers or programs. You would be surprised at how many items on your fixed expenses list can be modified. (Having eight hundred cable channels is a want, not a need.)

If that is not enough, you will need to consider living in a less expensive home or driving a less costly car. While this may result in a lifestyle change, to be financially secure, you have to follow your budget and live at a level that is within your means.

ACTIVITY: Discuss Your Budget with a Financially Savvy Person

Identify a friend or relative with your same income level or higher and discuss your budget with him or her. See how your two budgets compare. You may be surprised at how different your budgets are in certain categories. Are the differences in your budgets due to differences in lifestyles, or do you just need to adjust your budget? This activity will help you determine how much you really need to spend on certain items so that you can create a real, workable budget given your individual situation. For information on comparing your budget to budgets for similar households, see the Resources section at the end of this book.

USE MONEY MANAGEMENT SOFTWARE TO KEEP TRACK OF YOUR BUDGET

Creating and keeping track of a budget can be easier when you use money management software. There may be a learning curve for catching on to how it works, but once you learn, it can be an invaluable tool. The software can provide you with a graph that shows you where you are spending your money. This can be especially helpful to someone with ADD, because people with ADD tend to learn more easily with a visual tool. (You can learn more about money management software in chapter 5.)

If you are comfortable with a spreadsheet program, such as Microsoft Excel, you can use that, but money management software contains additional features that will save you time and help prevent mistakes. Often a great time to buy this software is around March and April, when many office supply stores put money management software on sale ahead of the April 15 tax deadline. For office supply store information, see the Resources section at the end of this book.

MONEY GOALS

Coming up with financial goals can help you stick to your budget. These goals are the things you would like to accomplish with your money in the near and distant future. People with ADD are very driven by rewards—immediate rewards being most effective, followed by future rewards. This is why when you keep your eyes on the prize (your goals), it is much easier to follow a budget.

ACTIVITY: Immediate, One-Year, and Five-Year Financial Goals

In this activity, you will determine what goals you would like to accomplish with your money in the immediate and not-so-immediate future. When you write down your goals, you are much more likely to accomplish them. This is especially true if you have ADD, since many people with ADD need to see something written out to make it more "real" to them.

Using your notebook, write down five financial goals you would like to achieve in each of the following periods—within a couple of months, within a year, and then within five years. Since people with ADD can have a tendency to shoot for sometimes unachievable goals, here are examples of realistic goals for each time frame:

Immediate Goals (within a couple of months)

- Develop and follow a budget.

- Put away 10 percent of each paycheck in savings.

- Open a college fund for your children (see chapter 10 for more information).

One-year Goals

- Pay off one or two credit cards.

- Have up to two months of emergency expenses in savings.

- Get taxes completed on time.

Five-year Goals

- Pay off car loan.

- Have no credit card debt.

- Have at least six months of emergency expenses in savings.

- Have enough money saved up to buy a big-ticket item and still have enough left in savings.

ACTIVITY: Make Steps for Achieving Your Goals

If you are feeling confident and would like to do more, you can write out steps in your notebook for achieving each of these goals. If this seems daunting, it's okay—only do it if you feel up to it. Setting steps for each goal might look like this:

Goal: Pay off my car loan.

Step 1: Refinance the loan.

Step 2: Review your household budget and see where you might be able to cut back.

Step 3: Pay a little extra on your loan each month.

Setting just two or three steps for each goal is recommended. If you select more than two or three steps, the ADD brain may get overwhelmed. It is also a good idea to set a target completion date for each of these steps. Review your completion dates with a friend to make sure those dates are realistic. Mark those dates on a calendar so you can check your progress and keep on schedule. Following up periodically is an important part of achieving your goals!

SUMMARY

In this chapter, you discovered the difference between needs and wants and between fixed and flexible expenses. You also learned how to create a budget, set financial goals, and stick with each of them. In the next chapter, you will learn how to curb impulsive spending without depriving yourself of the things you need.

CHAPTER 7

Spending

If you have ADD, you may have learned the hard way that you impulsively spend money. You may be a little too eager to use your credit cards or spend any available cash. You may also find that you don't take care of the items on which you've spent your hard-earned money, resulting in your spending even more money to replace damaged items. In this chapter, you will learn how to practice rational spending, take care of the stuff you already own, and be a smart consumer.

SPEND WITHIN YOUR MEANS

In chapter 6, you learned how to make a budget. Part of having a budget is learning what you can and cannot afford. When you "spend within your means," you make purchases that are in line with your budget and are realistic, that is, based on how much money you make. However, there are some items that may be worth spending extra on.

Things You Don't Want to Skimp On

While it is important to spend within your means, there is some truth to the saying, "You get what you pay for." There are things that you want to spend extra money on. The trick is being able to figure out what they are. Things worth spending extra money on include the following:

■ Medical insurance

- Medication

- Household appliances you will use frequently

- Items of clothing you will wear often

RETAIL THERAPY

People with ADD are more prone to anxiety and depression and may soothe their feelings of frustration and inadequacy by shopping. They are also more likely to celebrate events by going out and buying things to "reward" themselves. No matter what the reason, you may find that you spend more money than you originally intended—you may have issues with impulsive spending. Here are some reasons why this happens to people with ADD:

- Acting before thinking things through

- Immediate need to "soothe" bad feelings

- The illusion that you aren't spending "real" money (when using credit cards)

- Need for immediate rewards

- Temporary distraction

Keep in mind that while spending can make you feel better immediately, that feeling quickly wears off and is replaced by guilt and remorse. That guilt and remorse is intensified when you get your credit card bill and when your impulsive spending causes conflict with your partner or spouse. In chapter 8 you will learn that people with ADD have a higher rate of credit card debt; this is in part due to impulsive purchases.

PRACTICE RATIONAL SPENDING

Your goal is to practice *rational spending*—spending that is not driven by impulsivity. There are ways to curb your need to spend when under stress or feeling the itch of impulsivity.

ACTIVITY: Come Up with Low-Cost Activities

If you are feeling the impulse to spend money either at the mall or online, the most obvious solution is to avoid shopping altogether. Instead, channel your need to reward or soothe yourself by doing things that don't cost as much money (and don't add stuff to your house). Here are a few things that can reward or soothe you that don't cost a lot of money:

- Enjoying an outdoor activity
- Taking a relaxing bath
- Spending time with friends
- Going to a museum
- Seeing a movie

Check your newspaper, city or county calendar of events, or local chamber of commerce website for a list of free and low-cost activities in your town. That way you don't even need to spend money on gas! In your notebook, make a list of at least five free and low-cost activities, both for you and your family.

Don't Touch Anything at the Store

When you touch an item on a store shelf, you are much more prone to buy it (Wolf, Arkes, and Muhanna 2008). This is one of the reasons why retailers encourage you to "try before you buy": once you have physical contact with the item, you are much more likely to claim it as yours. So avoid any "try before you buy" deals, and keep your hands off that store shelf!

Get a Shopping Monitor

People with ADD are very influenced by the behavior of others around them, so if you have to go shopping, don't do it alone. Bring along a friend who is not a spender. Use this to your advantage. Tell your friend ahead of time that if you want to buy something, you need to talk it over with him or her first. Keep in mind that you want to ask a friend who is honest but gentle when giving an opinion.

ACTIVITY: Using Your Shopping Monitor Effectively

When you go out shopping with your "monitor," tell him or her to ask you the following questions to justify your purchase:

- Do you need this item or do you just want it?

- Do you already have one similar to it?

- When would you actually use or wear this item?

- Is there something of equal value that you are willing to sell or donate to cut down on the amount of clutter in your home?

After you answer these questions, your monitor can make a recommendation about whether you need to make the purchase. The goal of this activity is not to deprive yourself of things but to make realistic choices about where your money is going.

USE WHAT YOU HAVE

People with ADD like to change their surroundings and decor often. This can get expensive. But you may be surprised to find that you already have the items you need right there in your own home. Is there anything that would be good to decorate with that until now has been put aside? For example, you can regularly rotate pictures or art to give your home a new look.

The concept of using what you have even extends to grocery shopping. Instead of running out a few times a week to get things for dinner (which is not only expensive, but a waste of time), use a recipe website where you can do an ingredient search in which you type in what you have in your pantry and the site comes up with recipes that fit your criteria and provides ratings of those recipes. See "Recipe Lookup" in the Resources section at the end of this book for website addresses.

STATUS SPENDING

You may have experienced problems making friends because of your impulsivity or because you feel like you lack social skills. This is a common experience when you have ADD. This is also why people with ADD are more likely to buy things to impress people or make friends. You may think that this is a much easier way of getting people to like you since you have not had much success with social skills in the past. However, buying expensive things or gifts to elevate your social status not only doesn't work, it can also lead to big bills.

Remember that you are perfectly okay the way you are, even if you feel socially awkward at times (or all the time). Plus the people that you attract with expensive gifts may not be genuine friends. It's a tough reality to face. A better way to meet friends and hone your social skills is by joining community organizations through which you are more likely to meet genuine, long-lasting friends who have the same interests as you.

GAMBLING

People with ADD may be prone to developing *compulsive gambling*. This is when you have an uncontrollable urge to keep gambling, even after it has caused you to lose large amounts of money, destroyed your family, and cost you your job. People with ADD who gamble compulsively may have more difficulty delaying immediate gratification than either compulsive gamblers without ADD or people who have neither ADD nor compulsive gambling behaviors (Rodriguez-Jimenez et al. 2006). This means that it is even more difficult for someone with both ADD and compulsive gambling to stop their addiction. For information on seeking help for gambling, see the Resources section at the end of this book.

The Difference Between Gambling and Investing

If you've already read chapter 4 about investing, you may be wondering if there is any real difference between gambling and investing. Sure, there are some similarities—you are putting your money on the line without really knowing for sure how much you are getting back, and both activities involve a certain level of risk. The difference is that in gambling, you have a much higher chance of losing than winning. When you invest in stocks, mutual funds, and bonds, however, you are not gambling because you have a much better chance of getting a return on your money since these are much more stable and less volatile investments.

NEGOTIATE EFFECTIVELY

Many things in life are negotiable, but because of difficulties with self-esteem, people with ADD may have difficulty negotiating prices of items or the amount of their salary. This is because a person with ADD may not know what he or she is worth or may not feel deserving of a better deal. Here are some tips on how you can successfully negotiate with someone for what you want:

- State your needs or write them out beforehand so you can think about them and be able to give all of your strong points later when actually in a negotiation situation.

- See things from the other person's perspective. Understand where they are coming from and how you can address their particular concerns.

- Know your limits—for example, the most you are willing to pay. Determine ahead of time the point at which you will not agree to a deal. Then stick to that limit in the negotiation. If you hear information that changes your previous assumptions, ask for a moment to think about it—do not try to adjust your position and continue negotiating at the same time.

- Avoid getting confrontational—stay calm. It is business, not personal. If you let your emotions interfere with your negotiating, you seriously risk making a bad decision. If you find yourself getting emotional, excuse yourself to go to the bathroom or to get a drink of water. Or let the other person talk while you take a few deep breaths to regain your focus. Don't worry what the other person will think of you. Interestingly, people will often respect you more after you negotiate with them, if you do it calmly and rationally.

For more information on negotiation, see "Negotiating" in the Resources section at the end of this book.

TAKE CARE OF WHAT YOU HAVE

It can be easy for someone with ADD to lose their possessions, accidentally spill something on them, step on them, or do other types of damage to them. More than likely, you have firsthand experience of looking for an item only to discover that the crunching sound you just heard was your foot crushing it to pieces.

A simple rule to follow is this: "a place for everything, and everything in its place." However, this can be a challenge when you have ADD! Sometimes just aiming to keep things off the floor is a good start. This way you at least have less of a chance of performing a Godzilla-like move on one of your favorite possessions. Storing things in the place where you are most likely to use them also prevents you from buying the same item over and over.

Take care of your possessions by safeguarding your valuable items. For example, if you use a laptop in public places, keep it with you at all times. Even if you just have to step away for a few minutes, it is really worth it to pack everything up and take it with you. You can also get a security lock for your laptop. For more information, see "Laptop Security Locks" in the Resources section at the end of this book.

BE A SMART CONSUMER

Smart consumers are aware of the quality and price of an item they are buying. They are able to make wise decisions about the timing of a purchase and are aware of the tricks retailers use to make sales.

Know What You Are Buying

Before you buy an item, look in a consumer guide to see how it is rated on quality and performance. Consumer guides tell you about a product's performance in rigorous tests and can even tell you the rate of repairs associated with a particular brand. Taking time to research an item also gives you the time to decide if you really need it or not. See the Resources section at the end of this book for information on consumer guides.

Avoid Trial Offers

Do not sign up for trial offers such as getting a free six-month subscription to a magazine. When you sign up for a trial offer, you are also indicating that the company can charge your credit card after the trial period has ended. When you have ADD, you have a tendency to forget detail-oriented tasks like canceling your trial offer before it expires, so it will save you money in the long run to avoid trial offers altogether. Companies count on people forgetting to cancel after their free trial period, and it results in more revenue for them.

Avoid Extended Warranties

When you are buying an electronic item or appliance, you may be asked by a salesperson if you want to purchase an extended warranty. Don't buy one. You will usually wind up paying more for the extended warranty than you would for any possible repairs—the chance that an item will break within the first year you purchase it is fairly low. Besides, many manufacturers have a one-year warranty on their products, which is automatically included in the price of the item. In addition, the work of trying to get something covered under the extended warranty can cost you more time and money than just getting it repaired and paying for it yourself.

Salespeople and online merchants receive a commission for sales of extended warranties, so there is definitely an incentive for them to sell you an extended warranty. The only time you might want to make an exception to this rule is to purchase an insurance plan that replaces your cell phone in case it is lost or damaged. This happens more often to people with ADD!

Look into Bundling Services

You may be able to get your telephone, Internet, and cable services *bundled* by ordering these services with one company. Bundling can save you money if you use these services often, have high-speed Internet, or if you want high-definition cable or a lot of channels. It may not be such a deal if you use basic cable and only use your home phone occasionally. Bundling can also simplify your bill paying, because you will have all of these services on one statement. It is recommended that you thoroughly look over your statement to make sure the bundling prices and services you were quoted are accurate as stated on your bill. Contact your local telephone, cable, or Internet provider for more information.

Travel Costs

Beware of travel sites where you "bid" and pay in full for a plane ticket or hotel before finding out the location of your hotel or flight times. You could have a difficult time getting your money back if you cancel or need to reschedule your trip.

Use a trip-advisor website. On these sites, actual travelers rate hotels, restaurants, and attractions in each city. They also provide a summary of their experiences. Remember that even if your trip doesn't turn out exactly as you planned, travel mishaps can make for the best stories! For information on trip-advisor websites, see the Resources section at the end of this book.

Buying Clothing and "Cost per Wear"

If you buy clothing just because it's on sale but you never wear it, it's not really a bargain. Spend more on clothing if you know you are going to wear the item more often. Think of the "cost per wear." If you buy a $200 coat and you wear it almost every winter day, your cost per wear is much lower than if you buy a $25 coat and wear it once.

Many smart shoppers know that it is more important to have fewer good-quality pieces of clothing than a closet full of poorly made clothing. Here are some things to look for in good-quality clothing:

- Patterns and stripes should match and line up everywhere on the garment.

- Seams should be secure; check this by grabbing the fabric on either side of a seam and pulling it taut.

- The fabric should keep its shape even after you grab it, bunch it, and let it out.

- The clothing should be the correct size and not show any pulling of the fabric or tight spots—that's a sign the item's panels were not sewed together correctly.

Buy clothing that is classic rather than trendy. You will get much more use out of a nicely made pair of pants than the latest skirt in a wild print. Also keep in mind that accessories, such as jewelry, can really change an outfit—and buying accessories is usually much less expensive than buying new pieces of clothing. You can also check out consignment stores. These are stores where people sell their new or gently used clothing. You can find an affordable outfit that is not only up-to-date but also, in many cases, hardly worn. An online auction site can also have a great selection, but make sure there are plenty of pictures and sizing information provided before you bid.

You can save money by making sure you are buying clothes in the correct size and making sure you really like a piece of clothing before you buy it. People with ADD are less likely than others to return an item either because they cannot find the receipt or do not want to take the time and effort to return it.

Buying a Car

You may get a better deal on a car if you buy it toward the end of the month when salespeople are trying to meet their monthly selling quotas. Salespeople expect you to negotiate with them, so do not take the first price they offer. Even better is to figure out exactly what car you want and then call dealerships over the phone to negotiate a price. That way instead of having to walk away, you just hang up the phone and call another dealer in your area.

If you buy a used car, make sure it has a *clean title history*. This means that the car has not been involved in any major accidents, nor has it been damaged in a natural disaster, such as a flood or hurricane. See the Resources section at the end of this book for information on how to get a copy of a car's title history.

Many states have "lemon laws" that protect you in the event you buy a car and discover that it was built with defects. For more information on lemon laws and your state's lemon law contact information, see the Resources section.

CARRY ONLY THE CASH YOU NEED

When you have ADD, you may go through cash very quickly. You may almost feel like you must immediately spend the money you have in hand. One solution to running through your money is to take only a set amount of cash out on a weekly basis. Be realistic about the amount of cash you need. When you run out of money for that week, you are done spending.

Try to carry bills of $20 and smaller, as some people find themselves spending more when they carry bills in larger denominations. If you use an ATM, make sure it does not charge you an additional fee for withdrawals. See chapter 9 for more information on bank services.

Nickel-and-Diming

Keep track of the little ways you spend money—those daily cups of gourmet coffee add up, and you may be surprised at the total dollar amount you spend each month on it. A simple change like bringing your coffee from home can make a big difference in your available funds (most national coffee chains sell their coffee in grocery stores also). To see the proof of how much you are saving, put the money you would usually spend on coffee each day into a jar and then count it up at the end of the month. Stopping your $3-a-day coffee habit can equal a savings of $90 a month. Now to help put this into perspective, look up something online that costs $90: pretty unbelievable that it equals a month of coffee!

ACTIVITY: Keep Track of Your Cash Purchases for One Week

Using your notebook, write down what you spend in cash each day for one week. Write down the item and the dollar amount spent no matter how small or insignificant the amount. You can write down this information either right at the time of purchase or save your receipts and write it down at the end of the day. You can then throw out your receipts unless you need them for tax records. (See chapter 5 for more information on when to save receipts and when to throw them out.)

Now that you have kept track of your cash spending for a week, do you notice any patterns to your spending? Do you see any areas where you are not spending wisely? Sometimes it can be surprising to find that you actually *are* spending your money appropriately! Now that you are armed with this information on how you spend your cash, go back to chapter 6 and add this information to the budget you created in your notebook in order to make it more accurate.

SUMMARY

In this chapter, you learned about practicing rational spending, taming the spending monster, limiting your cash outflow, and taking care of what you already have. You also learned how to protect yourself as a consumer and how to take care of your belongings. You may already notice how good it feels to take control of your spending habits. In chapter 8, you will learn about how best to get a handle on your loans and other debts and how to reduce your debt as much as possible.

CHAPTER 8

Loans and Debt

Having ADD makes you more prone to being in debt. People with ADD either have greater loan debt or have more difficulty qualifying for loans due to their poor credit history than people without ADD (Barkley, Murphy, and Fischer 2008). They are also more likely to pay late fees because they forget to make loan payments.

CREDIT RATING

A *credit rating* is a number that represents the creditworthiness of a person. The most common is a Fair Isaac Corporation (FICO) score, which is a number between 300 and 850. Your credit rating is determined by your past and current credit history, including credit card and loan payments, any collection agency action against you, any late payments, and your current debts on loans and credit cards. This information is put into what is called a *credit report*. The quality of your credit rating can influence your chances of getting a credit card, mortgage, or loan. The higher your credit rating, the more likely you are to receive a loan or a lower interest rate on that loan. Your credit report can be requested by potential creditors (when you apply for a credit card, for example), insurance companies, companies with whom you have an existing credit account, and landlords in order to determine your ability to make payments on time and assess your risk as a consumer.

ADD and Your Money

Check Your Credit Report

The information on your credit report is collected and sold by companies called *credit-reporting agencies*. You should check your credit report at least once a year. There are three main credit-reporting agencies. Each year you are entitled by law to one free credit report from each agency. You can get your free credit report from all three agencies at once or from a different agency every four months. Review the reports for accuracy, especially if you are planning in the near future to apply for a credit card or loan. Contact the credit agencies immediately if you find inaccurate information on your credit report. See the Resources section at the back of the book for contact information for the credit agencies.

If there is a mistake on your credit report, take the following steps when writing to the credit-reporting agency:

- Give details about the incorrect item, including any identifying account numbers.

- Enclose copies of documents that prove that the listing on your credit report is a mistake, including a canceled check and/or statement of payment from the creditor.

The credit agency will investigate and let you know the results in about thirty days. However, if the credit agency has not corrected the error after thirty days, take the following steps:

- Write to the company again and state that this is the second time you are contacting them about the incorrect information on your credit report.

- Give the date you sent the first letter.

- Include a copy of your first letter along with any other documentation.

- Demand removal of the incorrect information or an explanation of why the incorrect information is still on your credit report.

It's really not necessary to use a service or an attorney to clear your credit report unless both the steps listed above have not resolved the issue and you have very clear proof (that is, documentation) that the credit agency is in error. For more information on disputing an error on your credit report, go to the Resources section at the end of this book.

104

CREDIT CARDS

Using a credit card can be addictive for people with ADD because credit cards are convenient, easy to use, and make it is easy to forget you are paying with "real" money. But using a credit card means you are taking out a loan—usually at a high interest rate. This means you are actually spending more money for something when you pay with a credit card than when you pay with cash (Prelec and Simester 2001).

While you may hear that you should only use your credit card in emergencies, this advice may not be realistic, especially considering today's state of technology. If you purchase any items online, you either need to use a credit card or an online payment system.

Credit card companies may offer you attractively low interest rates, but read the fine print—those interest rates can increase a lot if you miss a payment. In addition, having too many credit cards lowers your credit rating.

If you do get a credit card, ask for a very low limit—no more than $500; just because credit cards allow you to carry a balance doesn't mean you should. One way to keep track of your spending is to record the dollar amount of the item you purchased on a sheet of paper along with your current bank balance. This way you can subtract the purchase amount from the money in your checking account, making sure you have enough money to pay the credit card bill when it is due. You may prefer to use a debit card, which works the same way as a credit card for making purchases but automatically deducts the money from your bank account. You will learn more about the pros and cons of debit cards in chapter 9.

Find the Best Credit Card for You

Credit cards have different interest rates, and some charge annual fees. Others offer "cash back" on purchases. The ideal card for you is one that has no annual fee and has a rewards (or "cash back") program that gives you at least 1 percent of your total bill back in the form of airline miles, cash, or points. Spend your points on airline miles or gift cards, because they offer the best monetary value for your points. You can find information on where to research your credit card options under "Credit Card Comparison" in the Resources section at the end of this book.

If You Lose or Misplace Your Credit Cards

If you can't find your credit card, you may wonder if it's misplaced at home, lost, or stolen. If you are fairly certain you lost your credit card when you were out or that it has been stolen, you should cancel your credit card as soon as possible. The bank will issue you a new card. If you think you misplaced it at home, but you can't find the card within a reasonable amount of time, you should cancel your card and request a replacement card. Since you don't have the original card with you (it is lost, remember?), you will need to find bank contact information and your account number in order to cancel the card and receive a new one. If you prepared for this possibility by scanning, photocopying, and/or logging this information when you first received your credit card, you will not have to dig through papers to find this information. The quicker you can contact your credit card issuer, the better!

Once you report your cards lost or stolen, the credit card companies will issue you new cards. However, you will need to wait up to a few weeks until the new cards arrive. This is why it is important to have a second "backup" credit card that you keep in a separate location—not in your wallet. Now you just need to remember where you are keeping that second card!

ACTIVITY: Record Your Credit Card Information

Since you may be prone to losing things, make a photocopy or scan of the front and back of your credit cards when you first receive them and file these with your important papers. This way, you automatically have the bank contact and account information in case you lose the cards. Also record the following information for each of your cards. Use a separate piece of paper for this activity instead of your notebook, for security purposes. Store this information in a locked file cabinet or other secure location in your home.

- Type of credit card (Visa, MasterCard, American Express, etc.)

- Issuing bank

- Credit card number

- Expiration date

- Your name as written on the card

- Contact information for the bank (on the back of your card)

Now if you cannot find the photocopies or scans of your cards, you know that at the very least you have that information stored securely in your home.

LOANS

A *loan* is money that you borrow from a lender. You sign a contract promising to pay this amount of money, plus interest, back to the lender over a specific period of time. Usually when you are loaned money, you then make a monthly payment to repay the loan. *Interest* is kind of like a fee; it is the way a lender (a bank, for example) makes a profit off loans. When you get a loan, you want to make sure you have the kind of loan that allows you to pay off the balance of the loan at any time without any penalty.

Loan interest rates are usually fixed, even if you *default* (fail to make your payments), and generally are in the 5–15 percent range. Banks base loan interest rates on several factors, including the cost to them of obtaining the funds to loan; their current *loan portfolio* (the loans they already have); your *collateral* with the bank (cash or property you give the bank if you default on your loan); your credit score; the reason you want the loan; and the "intangible," which is your relationship with the bank and loan officer. Compare this to credit card interest rates. Credit card companies can change their interest rates dramatically depending on a number of variables, and their interest rates can climb to more than 30 percent. Consider taking out a bank loan at a lower, fixed interest rate and using that money to pay off credit card debt, which is at a much higher interest rate.

Payday Loans

When you are in a real cash crunch, you may be tempted to take out a *payday loan*, which is a short-term loan with extremely high interest. This lending process is referred to as *predatory lending*, because payday loan lenders prey on those who are in desperate need of cash. A payday loan is usually for a few hundred dollars and has an interest rate in the triple digits. It usually has to be paid back within two weeks.

Important: Avoid these loans at all costs. For more information on why you should avoid these loans, see "Payday Loan Caution" in the Resources section at the end of this book.

Student Loans

Students with ADD are less likely to have money saved up for education and may be *underemployed* (not employed to the full potential of their ability), resulting in lower income. Therefore, they may have to borrow more money in the form of student loans than college students or college graduates without ADD.

GOVERNMENT VS. PRIVATE LOANS

If you are going to college in the United States, you have two main options for student loans. You can get a Stafford Loan from the U.S. Department of Education or a private loan through a bank or finance company.

Stafford Loans come in two forms—subsidized and unsubsidized. *Subsidized loans* are based on financial need and will not *accrue* (gather) any interest while you are a full-time student. *Unsubsidized loans* are given regardless of financial need and do accrue interest while you are in school. After leaving school, you may have the option of entering a *loan forgiveness program,* whereby your loan is either partially or fully *forgiven* (canceled) in exchange for doing work in an underserved area after you graduate. For example, if you volunteer with AmeriCorps for one year, you may receive a stipend and your student loans may be partially forgiven. For more information on AmeriCorps and other loan forgiveness programs, see "Loan Forgiveness" in the Resources section at the end of this book.

Although you may be able to borrow more money with a *private loan* than with a Stafford Loan, you will most likely pay a higher interest rate with a private loan. These bank loans almost always accrue interest while you are in school and may be harder to qualify for than Stafford loans. You also do not have the option of a loan-forgiveness program with private loans.

There are other options for paying for school, including grants and scholarships. For more information on Stafford Loans, private loans, and other forms of financial aid for college students, see "Student Loans" in the Resources section at the end of this book.

Auto Loans

The best thing to do is to not have an auto loan at all. However, this is not always a possibility, especially if you have ADD and may not have saved up enough money to pay for a car in full. If you need an auto loan, there are ways to take less of a financial hit.

GET A BANK LOAN

If you get a loan through the car dealer, you will probably pay a higher interest rate than if you get a loan directly from a bank. Let's say you find a car that you want to purchase. You can go in person to the bank of your choosing or even apply online at the bank's website. If you hold an account at a particular bank, you may be able to get a lower interest rate.

BUY USED OR NEW?

While you may want the latest car, it may not necessarily be the most reliable car. Some cars of previous years are actually better performers in comparison to newer models. Make sure you check a consumer guide and do your research before even going to a car dealer or answering an ad. Look in a car-value book or go to an online car-value site to determine the appropriate value. Remember that when you buy a new car, it automatically *depreciates* (loses some of its dollar value) as soon as you drive it off the lot. For more information, see "Car Value Lookup" in the Resources section at the end of this book.

You want to buy a car that is within your means. The smaller your down payment, the higher your regular payments—and the more likely it will be that you will wind up *upside down* in your loan, meaning that you owe more money on your car than it is worth. You definitely want to avoid that situation.

LEASE OR BUY?

Car leases were created to allow you to "buy" a car with little to no money down. If you lease, you will pay each month for the value that the car lost that month (depreciation) plus an additional financing cost. However, when you lease a car, there are limits on your yearly mileage. You also have to keep the car clean—which can be a challenge if you have ADD. You do have the option of buying the car at the end of your lease.

Buying a car will usually cost you less money than leasing the same car, especially if you drive more than twelve thousand miles a year.

LIVING ARRANGEMENTS

Before you take the plunge into buying a home, the most important thing to determine is if you can afford the monthly mortgage payment. When looking at your budget, consider this payment to be a fixed expense, meaning that it does not vary from month to month. (For adjustable rate mortgages, be sure to include your higher payments in your budget.) Also take into account the cost of upkeep and other things like homeowners insurance and property taxes. While upkeep expenses, such as getting new storm windows, may be flexible expenses that vary from year to year, costs such as home-owners insurance and property taxes are fixed expenses. One of the ways you can determine if you can afford to do this is to review chapter 6 and then update your budget to reflect all the new fixed and flexible expenses that home ownership entails.

Do not buy a house just to prove that you are an adult. Buying a house doesn't automatically mean you have made a wise decision. Wise decisions come from thoroughly looking at what is in your best interest and following through with that course of action. Whether that results in owning a house or not, you will know you have made the right decision. Peace of mind is worth much more than any piece of real estate.

Refinancing

People refinance their mortgage for one of two reasons: to lower their monthly mortgage payments or to borrow more money using their property as collateral. When interest rates drop, refinancing your mortgage can lower your monthly payment and save you money. A general rule is that if the new interest rate will be at least two percentage points below your old one, you should refinance. *Refinancing your mortgage* just means that you are getting a new mortgage and are using that new money to pay off your old mortgage. If you have money left over after paying off your previous mortgage, you can use that money for any purpose you wish. However, remember that it is still a loan and you do have to pay that money back, plus interest. The *closing agent* (mortgage broker) will handle the payoff of your current mortgage and make all the necessary legal filings.

If you decide to refinance, you are more likely to have the new mortgage approved if you have the following:

- A credit score above 600

- A conforming mortgage (ask your mortgage broker for details if your home qualifies for a conforming mortgage)

- Your total debt payments for the current year (excluding your estimated refinanced mortgage) are less than 25 percent of your income for the same period

To find out more about mortgage refinancing, see the Resources section at the end of this book.

PAYING OFF YOUR DEBTS

If you have come into extra money, it is wise to pay off whichever of your debts has the highest interest rate. Then pay off the debt with the second-highest interest rate, and so on. If not paid down, your high-interest debt will grow by more than whatever you might make by investing that extra money.

Credit cards usually have the highest interest rates of any debts you have. Make sure you are making *at least* the minimum payment on each credit card. If you are having difficulty even doing that, you have a few options to pursue.

If you've gotten to the point where you can't make your minimum payments on your bills, your creditors will have your accounts turned over to a collection agency. It is the collection agency's job to get your payment. Here are some tips to make life easier if you are faced with collection agencies.

Arrange a Payment Plan

Call the creditor and arrange to pay a certain amount of your bill on a monthly basis. Creditors are much more understanding if you make an effort to pay them instead of ignoring your debt. However, creditors are not legally required to set up a payment plan for you, so another option is to contact a credit counseling agency.

Contact a Credit Counseling Agency

If you are so far in debt that you can't even make your minimum payments on your credit cards every month, consider contacting a credit counseling agency, such as the National Foundation for Credit Counseling (NFCC). See the Resources section at the end of this book for contact information. Beware of any "credit counselors" or agencies who make you pay a big fee up front or offer you a "too good to be true" scenario of repayment. Using credit counseling services may adversely affect your credit score, but filing for bankruptcy certainly affects your credit—for many years. You will learn more about bankruptcy later in this chapter.

Know Your Rights

In the United States, the Fair Debt Collection Practices Act provides rules that creditors and collection agencies must follow when attempting to collect money you owe them. The Fair Debt Collection Practices Act states the following:

- A collection agency can only call you between 8 A.M. and 9 P.M. in your time zone.

- A collection agency cannot contact anyone else about your debt except your attorney, if you have one. However, an agency is allowed to call people to determine your address and phone number; representatives of an agency are simply not allowed to discuss your debt or to volunteer the information that they are from a collection agency.

- You can stop a collection agency from calling you by writing a letter to the agency within thirty days of first contact, stating that you do not want the agency to contact you any further. The only contact an agency can make after that point is a letter stating that it has ceased contact with you.

- If you dispute the debt, you can mail a written request for verification of the debt, and the creditor must provide it to you within thirty days.

- A collection agency cannot threaten you with jail, use obscene language, use a false name, deposit a postdated check before the date written, make you accept collect calls, or collect any amount of money greater than the actual debt (unless allowed by law).

If you feel your rights have been violated, you can report the violation to the Federal Trade Commission (FTC). For FTC contact information and additional information, please see "Fair Debt Collection Practices Act" in the Resources section at the end of the book.

ACTIVITY: Keep Track of Your Creditors

If you owe money to more than one source, it can be overwhelming to figure out who you owe money to, how much you owe them, and what stage you are at in the repayment or negotiation process.

In your notebook, write down the following at the top of a page for each creditor:

- Name of one of your creditors

- Contact information for creditor

- How much money you owe

- Whether you have contacted this creditor or returned their calls

- Negotiated payment plan (if any)

- Date the payment was *fulfilled* (paid off)

Leave a couple of blank pages after each entry so that you can log each additional contact with that creditor, jotting down the date of contact, the name of the person you spoke to, and details of your conversation. If you seek the services of a credit counseling agency, you can just bring the notebook with you. It will make the counseling process much more efficient.

PLAN FOR EMERGENCIES

As you learned earlier in the book, people with ADD have difficulty planning ahead due to dysfunction in the frontal lobes of the brain. This can mean you have trouble saving for a retirement fund (as described in chapter 5); it may also mean you have no money saved up in case of an emergency.

Here are some emergencies for which you might need extra money:

- Medical expenses
- Travel due to family emergency
- Loss of a job

It is recommended that you have at least two months' worth of expenses or 10 percent of your yearly income in your savings account. This gives you a cushion until things get better. If you are going through a crisis, having enough money to get by for a couple of months gives you some peace of mind; it is one less thing that you have to worry about. You can have your bank withdraw money from your paycheck directly into your savings account in order to build up your emergency fund. See chapter 9 for more information on direct deposit.

Note that it is best to pay off credit cards and other high-interest debt before starting an emergency fund. Once you do begin building your emergency fund and have two months' worth of expenses saved, shoot for increasing your emergency fund to six months' worth of expenses.

Using Investments for Emergency Use

If you have investments, you can use them for an emergency—but it is much better to use up your cash savings first. If you have run out of savings, you can take out a loan from your 401(k) for up to five years. You could take money out of your IRA but you would pay a 10 percent penalty plus income taxes on those withdrawals. The only way to avoid paying this penalty is if you can prove financial hardship to the IRS, if you are using the money to pay for college expenses, or if you are taking out up to $10,000 for a first-time home purchase. **Important:** there are restrictions that apply. See your financial professional for further information on these restrictions. For information on 401(k) plans and IRAs, see chapter 3.

Liquidating

You may have seen a store with the sign "Liquidation—Going-out-of-Business Sale." This means the store is selling goods for cash before closing its doors permanently. If you truly need money quickly, you can also do a liquidation of some of your belongings.

Due to impulsivity, you may jump the gun on needing to liquidate, so before you take the extreme step of selling your investments or valuable items, ask yourself the following questions:

- Is this emergency situation temporary or permanent?

- Will I benefit from the cash more than I will regret selling the item?

- Does the item I want to sell have value to future generations and/or sentimental value?

- Will selling this item cause resentment or anger in my family members or friends?

- Will selling this item cause me more relief than pain?

- A year from now, do I see myself being happy or relieved about selling this item?

When you have ADD, it can be difficult to look at the impact that decisions you make now will have on your future—make sure you weigh all your options before you sell valuable investments or items in your home. Before you make such a weighty decision, consider consulting with a financial professional. (See chapter 4 for information on financial professionals.)

However, selling inexpensive items and items of no sentimental value not only gets you some extra cash but also clears some clutter out of your house and does a good turn for the environment by reducing your trash. And if you have ADD, the less clutter you have, the better you will feel.

ACTIVITY: What Can You Sell?

What are some items that you don't really use and could make some money from? If you have an item in mind, look at an online auction site to see what a similar item is selling for. In your notebook, write down each item you're considering and its estimated value (obtained by doing online research or by getting the item appraised). If you do want to sell this item, decide if you would rather sell it at a garage sale (best for lower-valued items), on an online auction site, or through an ad.

BANKRUPTCY

Bankruptcy is a legal process in which your debts are eliminated by selling most of your assets or by making on-time payments under a court-ordered payment plan. You should consider bankruptcy to be a last resort, as it will make it very difficult for you to get credit for many years and your credit score will fall hundreds of points. You will live a cash-only existence, which means your utilities will need to be prepaid and/or will require deposits, and you will have to have cash or use a checking account if you want to buy anything.

So how do you know if you need to consider bankruptcy? You should consider it if this is your status:

- Your *liabilities* (money owed) greatly exceed your assets.

- You experience severe financial distress due to a major life event, such as an unexpected job loss or medical condition.

- You have already met with a credit counseling agency, followed their recommendations, and are still in severe debt.

- You have exhausted all other means of paying your debts.

Bankruptcy is a big decision, so make sure you consider all your options before you make up your mind. Contact a bankruptcy attorney and have an introductory consultation. You can find a bankruptcy attorney by asking for referrals from trusted family and friends. Make sure the attorney specializes in bankruptcy law. You can also contact your state's bar association to see if it certifies attorneys in bankruptcy law.

SUMMARY

In this chapter, you learned how having ADD can affect your credit score, ability to get a loan, and chances of having a high amount of debt. You also learned about different types of loans as well as ways you can protect yourself in the event that you owe money and are lacking the funds. In chapter 9, you will learn about bank services that can simplify your money management practices.

CHAPTER 9

Bank Services

Banks offer a wide variety of services and conveniences. But they also can charge a lot in fees, which can really add up over time. You may not be aware of some banking options that are particularly useful to people with ADD. In this chapter, you will learn what bank services are available and how to find a bank that is best for your needs.

TYPES OF ACCOUNTS

Nearly everyone has a checking account, and many people also have savings accounts or certificates of deposit. *Checking accounts* allow you to write checks and use debit cards, but they pay little to no interest and often have a monthly fee. *Savings accounts* pay a better interest rate and are usually free but do not allow you to write checks. *Certificates of deposit* (CDs) are like savings accounts except you earn a slightly higher interest rate and your money cannot be withdrawn for a specified period of time unless you pay a penalty fee.

BANK SERVICES

Your bank can offer you various services that can make financial management much easier for a person with ADD. These services can save you time and cut down on the amount of paper that accumulates on your desk. Bank services include overdraft protection, direct deposit, automatic withdrawal, debit cards, and automatic teller machines.

Overdraft Protection

People with ADD are more likely to pay bank fees because of low balances in their checking accounts or *overdrafting* (writing checks when there isn't enough money in the account to cover them). Open an account in a bank that offers overdraft protection for minimal or no fee. *Overdraft protection* means that, if you accidentally write a check or use your debit card when you don't have enough money in your checking account, the bank will automatically transfer the needed money from your savings account (provided you have enough money in savings). Even if you pay a small penalty fee, this is worthwhile because the charge for writing a check that bounces can be quadruple what you would pay for an over-draft transfer. Using overdraft is always better than having the embarrassment, lack of trust, and legal problems you might encounter if your check bounces.

Another reason to have overdraft protection is that some banks process deposits and withdrawals in a way that causes you to be overdrawn. Banks make a lot of money from overdraft fees—a nationwide total of $1.97 billion in 2006 (Federal Deposit Insurance Corporation 2008). Banks process withdrawals throughout the day but they only process deposits at the end of the day. They may also process the largest withdrawal first and then the smaller ones, in this way increasing the number of times you pay an overdraft fee (Consumer Federation of America 2008; Grant 2007). These business practices vary greatly between banks, so be sure to ask about this when you are inquiring about overdraft protection. Ask the bank officer you deal with how the bank processes withdrawals and deposits each day so you can better understand the need and expected cost of overdraft protection. If the bank will provide you with a bank policy statement in writing, that is useful, but these can be difficult to read so make sure the bank officer explains it to you.

Direct Deposit and Automatic Withdrawal

If you have ADD, you may be prone to misplacing your paycheck, forgetting to deposit it, or cashing it and spending all the money. Direct deposit solves these problems. There's no paper check to deal with because the amount of your paycheck is electronically deposited directly into your checking account. You can also tell the bank to put a percentage or dollar amount of your paycheck into your savings account automatically each month. You will be saving money without having to do a thing!

Automatic withdrawal is a great way to avoid late fees and save time. Contact the companies that send you regular bills, such as utilities and credit cards, and ask them if they will deduct directly from your checking account.

Important: The trick is to make sure you have enough money in your checking account at the time that the withdrawal is scheduled.

To help with that, try to arrange your withdrawals to occur a few days after your paycheck gets deposited. Most companies will let you pick the day (such as the fifteenth of the month) for the automatic withdrawal. You also need to make sure that companies with which you have discontinued services are not continuing to withdraw money out of your account. Check your bank statements for these withdrawals for a few months to make sure the payment isn't still being withdrawn from your account.

ACTIVITY: Who Can I Pay Automatically?

In your notebook, write a list of your recurring monthly expenses and the companies they come from. Then research each company to see if it offers automatic bill pay. Many times this information is given on the company's web page. Some companies, such as auto insurance companies, will even let you pay monthly without a finance charge! Companies that may offer automatic payments include the following:

- Auto insurance
- Internet
- Cell phone
- Telephone
- Utilities

Once you determine which companies offer automatic payments, sign up for the services online, or call the company for more information.

Debit Cards

Think of a debit card as an electronic checkbook. When you use it, money is pulled out of your checking account immediately. Debit cards are convenient, very helpful for people who have poor credit or money management skills, and safer than carrying around a lot of cash. However, as with your real checkbook, if your debit card is stolen, you may be responsible for some or all of the thief's purchases. Because debit cards withdraw money automatically from your account, you have to keep track of your account balance in your checkbook.

Important: Be especially cautious about using your debit card to purchase things online. Using a credit card is a wiser choice because you can more easily dispute unauthorized charges with your credit card company (the money hasn't already been taken out of your checking account) than you can with your bank for a debit card withdrawal.

LIMIT YOUR USE OF AUTOMATIC TELLER MACHINES

Getting cash quickly can be a very useful and convenient thing, but it is also a big temptation if you have ADD. The more money that is available to you, the more likely you are to spend it. If you do use an ATM, make sure it is one that does not charge an additional fee for withdrawals. Check with your bank to find out which ATMs are "approved" and do not charge you extra.

REMEMBERING YOUR PIN

It seems that you need more and more PINs (personal identification numbers) and passwords each day. If you have difficulty remembering stuff, it can be really tough to remember a combination of four numbers. **Important:** Do not use your birthday, street address, name, or the series "1, 2, 3, 4" as your PIN or password. There are websites that will store your PINs and passwords. You just need one password to access the account. Make sure the website uses encryption technology for added security. See "Password and PIN Storage" in the Resources section at the end of the book for information on these websites.

ACTIVITY: Can Someone Guess Your PIN?

Empty out your wallet or purse right now. Is your PIN/password somewhere on one of the cards, photos, or notes in front of you? Maybe it is your child's name, a street number, birth date, street address, or phone number. If a thief has your wallet or purse, these things might help him or her to guess your PIN/password. If there's a connection between the items you carry and your PIN/password, change it or leave that identifiable item at home.

BANK FEES

Fees are a part of banking, and to some degree banks couldn't exist without them. However, bank fees have increased over the years. In 1996, bank fees were 3 percent of bank income; in 2006 they were 56 percent at $80 billion (Grant 2007). Here are some of the things that might incur bank fees:

- Low account balances

- Average-to-heavy check writing

- Teller deposits

- Overdraft protection

- ATM fees

- Check printing

People with ADD are more prone to paying these fees because of forgetfulness or difficulty keeping track of an account balance. Your goal is to find a bank with the service and features you need and with few-to-no fees.

FINDING THE RIGHT BANK FOR YOU

Finding the right bank for your needs is like finding a good business partner. The closer the bank you choose is to meeting your needs and lifestyle, the better your banking experience will be. Banks really do vary quite a bit from each other. Useful banking services, number of branches, convenience, fees, and customer service are just some of the key areas in which banks differ.

Traditional Banks vs. Credit Unions

Since people with ADD usually pay more banking fees than other people, consider having your accounts at a credit union. Credit unions generally have lower bank fees and allow lower balances in your accounts than traditional banks. However, not everyone can join a credit union, as by law they are limited to people who share a common employer (military, public school systems, hospitals, etc.), live in a certain geographic area (a local neighborhood credit union), are members of a particular nonprofit group (alumni groups, churches, etc.), or share the same profession (teachers, students, doctors, etc.). Credit unions and their services differ greatly from one another, so ask plenty of questions to see if a particular credit union is best for you.

Know Your Banking Needs

The first requirement in selecting a bank is finding one that is FDIC insured (or NCUSIF insured, for credit unions). Most banks are, but it's still good to confirm, as this means the federal government will protect your money, up to a certain dollar amount, if anything happens to the bank.

Next, ask yourself what you plan to do with your money. Do you just want to keep it there to grow safely? If so, the interest rates offered are important to you. Will you be writing a small or large number of checks? If you will be writing a large number, you will want to have free or low-cost checking. Do you also plan to use the bank for your business accounts? If so, you need a bank that can provide services tailored to your business as well as your personal needs. And if you need a loan, finding a bank that understands your situation or business may be the most critical factor.

CONSIDER BANK CONVENIENCE

When you are thinking about the bank services you might need, consider the convenience of the bank. Do you need to visit the bank on evenings or weekends, or do you prefer banking online with an easy-to-use website? Finding a bank that fits your lifestyle and preferences is important to people with ADD, since you may want to use the bank outside of normal business hours or you may want a bank that is convenient to you so that you are more likely to make your bank deposits.

ACTIVITY: Select the Right Bank

To help you identify the best bank for you, here is a list of various bank services. In your notebook, write the three to five items from the following list that are most important to you, and then compare that list to what your current bank offers to see how well it meets your needs.

■ Free checking

- High-interest accounts
- Easy-to-use online banking
- Free check printing
- Safe deposit boxes
- Evening and/or weekend hours
- Free or low-cost overdraft protection
- Convenient branch offices
- Face-to-face service
- Bank employees who know who you are
- Recommended by friends or relatives
- Large ATM network
- No/low ATM fees
- Offers mortgage loans
- Offers auto loans
- Offers small-business loans
- Out-of-state branches
- International branches
- ATMs

Move Your Accounts to One Bank

Many people find that, over time, they have scattered their bank accounts among various banks. They may have a checking account with one bank, a CD in another, and a mortgage with a third. Since banks tend to view all of your accounts together to determine the fees you should be charged, you may save money by consolidating all of your accounts with one bank. It is also easier for a person with ADD to keep track of his or her accounts when they are all kept at one location! When talking to a bank officer about opening up an account, describe the accounts you have with other banks and ask if you would receive any benefits if you transfer those accounts to this one bank.

SUMMARY

In this chapter, you learned about bank services, including overdraft protection, debit cards, direct deposit, and automatic withdrawal. You also discovered how to find the best bank for your needs. In chapter 10, you will learn how to talk to your children about money.

CHAPTER 10

Talking to Your Kids About Money

ADD has a heritability rate of 75 percent. That means if you have ADD, there's a 75 percent chance it was caused by inherited genes (Rietveld et al. 2004). It also means that there is a very good chance that your child has symptoms of ADD too. In fact, it may be that you didn't discover you had ADD until your child was diagnosed with it.

You and your child may have the same issues with money: impulsive spending, difficulty keeping track of money, and other pitfalls. In this chapter, you will learn how to improve your child's (and in turn, your) relationship with money.

Just because you have had financial challenges does not mean that your child is resigned to the same fate. In fact, your life experiences make you an even better teacher for your child! Something positive *can* come out of your years of struggling with money.

ISSUES WITH ADD CHILDREN AND MONEY

Having a child with ADD can present specific money challenges not very different from the money issues you may experience yourself. Challenges include dealing with impulsive spending, disorganization with finances, and spending money to impress friends. The tendency to spend money to impress friends may be even more intense for ADD children than for adults due to peer pressure and a child's strong need to feel accepted.

EXPLAINING MONEY TO CHILDREN

Keep in mind that children with ADD usually lag a little behind other children of their age when it comes to learning and processing information. Have your children sit with you while you work on your money management software, write checks, or look over your investments in the newspaper or online. The more your children are exposed to the day-to-day workings of money, the better. You can even have your child "pretend buy" stocks and track how the prices of those stocks go up and down.

Open a Savings Account for Your Child

Start teaching your child from a young age about how banks and bank accounts work. Go with your child to the bank and open up a savings account in his name. The bank will also put your name on the account as *custodian*. This means that the main account holder is a child, but you have full access to the account. You can make deposits and withdrawals and close the account.

Your child will have a sense of pride when putting allowance or birthday money into an account with his name on it. You can show your child the account statements each month. You can also teach your child about how money earns interest and how to follow the account online and with money management software.

Play Money Games

Playing board games (like Monopoly) that involve money teaches children about spending and buying. Children with ADD can be competitive, which actually enhances their learning process when playing such a game. Make sure you take turns quickly—otherwise your child (and possibly you) may become bored with the game. Also, since children with ADD have difficulty with multistep directions, make sure the game is at the child's learning level and has simple instructions. Some board games have a version especially designed for younger children.

Show Children the Bigger Picture

If you are in Washington, DC, or Fort Worth, Texas, you can take a tour of the U.S. Bureau of Engraving and Printing, where paper currency is made. If you are in Denver, Colorado, or Philadelphia, Pennsylvania, you can take a tour of the U.S. Mint, where coin currency is made. Children (especially ones with ADD) love seeing how things are made. Showing them how money is made makes a lasting impression and instills a sense of respect for it. For more information on the U.S. Bureau of Engraving and Printing and the U.S. Mint, see the Resources section at the end of the book.

Should You Talk About Your Salary with Your Child?

It is recommended that you tell your child about your job and even take her with you to work (if possible). However, it is not recommended that you tell your children how much money you make, even if they ask. Remember, whatever information you tell your children, it can be shared with other children. A good rule to follow is, "Would I want my child sharing this information with children on the playground?"

INVOLVE YOUR TEENAGERS IN SOME FINANCIAL DECISIONS

People with ADD, especially young people, learn best by actively participating in an activity. Involving your teenagers in some money decisions will help make the idea of earning money much more personal and memorable.

You could meet once a month after dinner for a financial meeting. This is usually the best time to get everyone in the family together. Also, you can tell your teenager to call a meeting if he gets a financial idea. This encourages your teen to take initiative and think more about money issues. A parent should be the leader of the meeting to help keep the discussion on topic and productive. Your family can vote to make some financial decisions, and it is recommended that a majority of your family vote to approve (or not approve) a decision. Children need to feel like they have a meaningful impact, so if something can be delegated to them, like overseeing a small investment or selecting an item to purchase, they will feel like they are part of the process. Your teenagers can be involved in family decisions such as the following:

- Choosing whether to lease or buy a new car

- Setting a vacation budget

- Making periodic investment reviews

- Making home improvement or move decisions

Use your own comfort level as a guideline for appropriate topics. In the following activity, you will be given a format for involving your teenager in a family meeting about money.

ACTIVITY: Blueprint for a Money Discussion

When you involve your teenager in a family discussion about money, it helps to have a set format. This is especially useful if both you and your child have ADD and are prone to getting off track. Appoint one person to be the note taker at your meeting. That person will fill out the following information in your notebook:

Topic of meeting:

Who brought up this topic?

Why is this topic important?

Your opinion:

Teen's opinion:

Final decision:

Why was this decision chosen?

Meetings will become easier and easier the more you use this format.

TALKING TO YOUR CHILD ABOUT MONEY TROUBLES

It is estimated that 1.95 million children will lose their homes due to foreclosure in 2008 and 2009 (Lovell and Isaacs 2008). Due to the increased number of home foreclosures and the weak economy, you may find yourself unexpectedly having to explain to your children why you are moving, why you can't afford things you could afford before, or why you are now at home during the day instead of going to work.

You may think that your child is not aware of your financial struggles and that you may be able to act as if everything is fine. However, even if children don't pay attention when asked to do their chores, they are very perceptive about what is going on within their family. Children with ADD seem to be particularly good at picking up information from conversations they overhear.

Children experiencing the loss of their home have stress and anxiety, just like adults. In fact, children and adolescents with ADD can be more sensitive and more prone to anxiety and depression than non-ADD children (Biederman, Ball et al. 2008; Brunsvold et al. 2008; Bowen et al. 2007). They may be more upset than the average child about your family's financial situation.

Be sure to ask your children what they have questions about. When you talk to your child, keep in mind that children usually just want a simple explanation. There's no need to go into great detail. In fact, too much detail can cause more anxiety for your child. Also, when talking to a child with ADD, gear your answer to her developmental rather than actual age since, as you learned earlier in this chapter, children with ADD may be closer to the emotional level of a younger child.

ACTIVITY: Come Up with a Script for Talking to Your Child About Money

Your child may ask the following questions about your financial situation:

- Are we going to move?

- Do I have to go to a different school?

- Will I still be able to see my friends?

- A child at school said we are poor. What does that mean?

- Mommy/Daddy has been upset and crying. Why?

- Are we going to be okay?

- Should I sell my toys since we need money?

In your notebook, write down how you would answer these questions. Keep in mind your child's age and his ability to understand information.

Review your answers to these questions with your spouse or another older family member. It is important that both parents agree on these answers.

When writing your answers, emphasize that you will make sure that your child will be safe during this time and that the problems you are having now have nothing to do with your love for one another. In fact, you can point out that it is more important than ever to treat everyone in the family with kindness and love. You can also stress that many children and parents are going through the same thing right now so that your child does not feel so alone. Think of how you would have liked your parents to answer these questions when you were your child's age.

USE ALLOWANCE AS AN INCENTIVE AND TEACHER

It is recommended that your child earn an allowance by doing chores around the house instead of just being given a specific dollar amount each week. Money is a powerful motivator, especially for children with ADD. And by paying your children for chores, you are actually saving yourself time by not needing to ask three times to get your child to start a chore!

In addition, earning something through hard work is great for a child's self-esteem. If a child earns an item by doing chores, never take that item away as part of a consequence. If you do punish a child by taking away an item she has earned, your child is less likely to try to earn rewards in the future. Your child may think, "Why bother doing this chore again? Mom and Dad can just take away my reward anyway."

You may be asking yourself, "Isn't giving rewards just a way of 'bribing' my child?" or maybe, "Why should children be paid to do what is expected of them?" An obvious answer to this is, "You get paid to go to work, don't you?" Having children earn things gives them an idea of what the "real world" is like. You can't just walk into your boss's office and say, "Hey, I don't feel like working today. Just pay me instead."

Children with ADD respond especially well to positive reinforcement. So why not make life easier for you (and your child) by using rewards?

Choose Appropriate Chores

For a more successful chore and allowance process, make sure you assign chores that are appropriate for your child's age or developmental level. The chore should be realistic and something that can be completed fairly easily by your child. The following chores are recommended:

Six to Ten Years Old

- Carry in the groceries.

- Set the table for dinner and then clear it. **Important:** Use unbreakable dishes and cups since children with ADD are accident prone.

- Hang up clothes in the closet.

- Hang up towels in the bathroom.

- Give food and water to pets.

Eleven to Seventeen Years Old

- Pack his or her own suitcase.

- Weed the yard. **Important:** Because of impulsivity and possibly poor motor coordination, children and teens with ADD should not perform chores with machinery, such as mowing the lawn, or any other chore that could potentially cause injury.

- Load and unload the dishwasher.

- Answer the phone and take messages.

- Buy items at the grocery store.

Before you ask your child to do a chore, make sure the chore consists of only one or two steps. Children with ADD have difficulty completing multistep tasks. Make sure you do the chore with your child all the way through at least a few times and write down each step of the chore. For more information on appropriate chores and allowance for children, see the Resources section at the end of this book.

How Much Should I Pay My Child for Chores?

How much you pay your child for each chore depends on your financial means, the child's age, and the complexity of the chore. This is where a budget, as described in chapter 6, can really help you figure out how much you can afford per chore.

The important thing is not so much that you set a dollar amount, but that you and your child come to an agreement together. Negotiating a dollar amount per chore is also a valuable experience for your child. You will learn later in this chapter about the importance of giving your child a say in his chores and allowance. You can also read in chapter 7 about the importance of learning negotiating skills.

What Constitutes a "Completed Chore"?

Children with ADD are not the best at doing a chore thoroughly and completely. Before criticizing or denying your child allowance or a reward for what you view as an incomplete job, make sure you talk to your child (and have her repeat back to you) the steps that needed to be done for this chore to be completed successfully. As mentioned before, chores that only have one or two steps to complete are best. If your child did not understand the steps—even after first completing the chore with you and then writing out the steps—consider if the chore is too complicated for your child's developmental level. Rarely do children intentionally want to displease their parents.

One of the symptoms of ADD is having difficulty learning from mistakes, so try to refrain from getting frustrated if your child makes the same mistake over and over again. Also look at your standards. Is it possible that you are expecting too much from your child? Keep in mind, as was mentioned earlier, that developmentally, your child's behavior may be that of a child two-thirds his actual age.

ACTIVITY: Creating a Chore Chart

Using a weekly calendar format, list which chore is to be done on each day. You can find resources for creating chore charts in the Resources section at the end of this book. Then put a star next to the chores that were completed. This way your child has a clear idea of how much she has accomplished. Without a visual record, it can be easy for children with ADD to forget how much they have accomplished, and they can lose sight of their goals. Now post the chore chart on the refrigerator so everyone sees it.

Rules About Rewards

You will improve the chances of chore-completion success if your child chooses his own rewards. You may be concerned that he may choose something like "a trip to Disney World," but children usually come up with pretty realistic rewards. You may even find that the reward your child chooses is much smaller than you expected.

Children and adults with ADD thrive on immediate rewards. When your child completes a chore successfully, give her the allowance payment right then and there. If you give the money later on, your child won't connect her hard work with earning the money. Have your child put the allowance in a jar. Once the jar is full, your child can spend it on the item of her choice, you can put the money into your child's savings account, or you can do both. It is recommended that your child get at least one item with this allowance, to make her effort seem more "real." Children, especially those with ADD, need to actually see something to know they have earned it.

As you learned earlier in the chapter, children with ADD are prone to impulsive spending, just like adults with ADD. While you can gently guide children toward the best way to spend their allowance, making the decision about what to purchase is ultimately up to them. They may learn quickly whether the item they bought was a wise choice or if it would make more sense to save up for a bigger item later.

When Rewards Don't Work

Some children with ADD are immune to rewards, just like some people are immune to certain illnesses. You can offer the best reward possible, and your child may just totally refuse it. This can be the case, especially with children who have an oppositional streak. What do you do if this happens? First, make sure your child has had a say in the chores and rewards. Also make sure that the chores and dollar amounts you've assigned to them are realistic.

If you've done these things, and your child still isn't moved by a reward, you can have your child earn *time* to do the things he likes in exchange for doing chores. This also works in cases where you do not have extra money to give your children for chores. All children like something: playing video games, for example. If you child does the chores, he gets to use the video game system for a certain amount of time—no chores done, no video game time. If you institute this rule, make sure you keep the video game system out of reach. ADD children can be really creative in finding out where you've hidden something. After children have been subjected to this "earn to play" routine, it's amazing how quickly they change their minds about doing chores for money!

THE BENEVOLENT DICTATORSHIP OF PARENTING

Your role as a parent is one of the "benevolent dictator." Pick your battles wisely. Don't abuse your power and crush a child's idea just because you can or because you need to show your child "who is boss." Remember, though, that you do have the final say. You do what you determine is in the best interest of your child, which means giving praise and enforcing consequences. However, the "benevolent" part means that you still listen to your child's input, such as what rewards they would like or the dollar value of a particular chore.

Seriously take into consideration your child's recommendations or your child will learn that his or her opinion doesn't count. If you have to say no to a reward, try not to present it as, "There's no way we can afford that reward!" Instead, try, "That may be a little pricey for us right now, so let's talk about a reward that is similar to that but may cost a little less." This approach makes children feel that you are taking their opinions into account and are willing to work with them.

SAVING UP FOR COLLEGE

While you certainly aren't required to save up money for your child's college education, it is a good idea to make the effort. Every little bit of money saved for tuition helps your child avoid the student loan debt trap. Roughly 66 percent of graduating college seniors have student loan debt, at an average of $19,300 per student (U.S. Department of Education 2004). In addition, children who receive financial help from their parents during college may have better money management skills and have fewer financial difficulties while in school than those who do not receive parental help and who support themselves solely through a job, student loans, or their own savings (Worthy, Blinn-Pike, and Jonkman 2008). Saving money for your child's college tuition shows your child that you are financially and emotionally invested in his or her education.

529 Plans

There is an account that is designed to help you save for your child's future education. A *529 plan* is a type of investment account run by each individual state. You deposit money into an account, usually monthly. You can set up electronic withdrawals from your bank account to go into the 529 plan. (See chapter 9 for more information on banks and electronic withdrawal service.) The money you contribute to this account cannot be deducted from your federal taxes, but it may be deductible from your state taxes. It is recommended that you consult a financial professional for specific questions about 529 plans.

There are two types of 529 plans: savings and pre-paid. The *savings plan* increases (or decreases) in growth based on the performance of its investments. These plans are administered by states and sometimes run by brokerages. With a *pre-paid* 529 plan, your child's future tuition is "locked in" at the dollar amount it was the year you started the account. You are "purchasing" tuition credits at today's prices. This is to your advantage, because the cost of tuition usually increases each year. You can also decide whether you want to put money into the 529 plan for tuition only or for tuition and housing. Pre-paid plans can be administered by states or by colleges and universities. Every state's 529 plan is different, especially in regard to the early withdrawal of funds or availability of funds if your child goes to college out of state. Given the current economy, some states may not be able to pay out the full amount of tuition from pre-paid tuition plans (Koba 2009). Meet with your financial adviser if you have any questions. See the Resources section at the end of this book for more information on 529 plans.

You can review the 529 plan statements with your child. This teaches your child about investing and makes it clear that you have worked hard to put her through college. This can help support your child's seriousness and stick-to-itiveness when she does go to college. Knowing you have invested the money makes it more likely that your child, in turn, will invest more time and effort in studies. It can also help your child make a decision about which college to attend—an in-state school where tuition is already covered thanks to your investment or a private school where tuition costs up to tens of thousands of dollars a year.

SUMMARY

In this chapter, you learned about how to instill in your child a sense of mastery about money, regardless of your own history with money management. You learned that your child can have a successful financial future even if he or she has ADD. You also discovered the importance of saving up for your child's college education and learned about an investment account designed especially for this purpose.

Conclusion

In this book, you have learned some basic financial concepts and methods for successful money management. Even if you have a history of disorganization and of doing things impulsively, you can use these methods to improve your financial discipline and stick to your financial plan. Continue your learning by reading and talking with others to improve your financial decision making, and turn your goals into reality. The sky's the limit!

Resources

Background Checks

CASAnet
Statewide Criminal Background Check Resources
www.casanet.org/program-management/volunteer-manage/criminal-bkg
-check.htm

Intelius
www.intelius.com

US Search
1-800-US-SEARCH (1-800-877-3272)
www.ussearch.com

Banking and Insurance Information

Federal Deposit Insurance Corporation
www.fdic.gov

Budget Comparison Tool

CNNMoney.com
Instant Budget Maker
http://cgi.money.cnn.com/tools/instantbudget/instantbudget_101.jsp

Car Title Information

CarFax
www.carfax.com

Car Value Lookup

Edmunds
www.edmunds.com

Kelley Blue Book
www.kbb.com

Chores and Children

Chore Charts
www.chorecharts.com

DLTK's Custom Chore Chart
www.dltk-cards.com/chart

Family Education
http://life.familyeducation.com/allowance/jobs-and-chores/34438.html

Consumer Advocate

Clark Howard Show
www.clarkhoward.com

Consumer Guide

Consumer Reports Magazine (from Consumers Union)
1-800-879-9848
www.consumerreports.org

Consumers Union
1-914-378-2000
www.consumersunion.org
101 Truman Avenue
Yonkers, NY 10703-1057

Consumer Rights and Information

Consumer Federation of America
1-202-387-6121
www.consumerfed.org
1620 I Street, NW
Suite 200
Washington, DC 20006

Credit Card Comparison

BankRate.com
www.bankrate.com/credit-cards.aspx

Credit Card Guide
www.creditcardguide.com

Credit Counseling

National Foundation for Credit Counseling
www.nfcc.org

Credit Rating Bureaus

Equifax
1-800-685-1111
www.equifax.com

Experian
1-888-397-3742
www.experian.com

TransUnion
1-800-888-4212
www.transunion.com

Credit Report

Annual Credit Report
www.annualcreditreport.com

Credit Report Dispute

Kiplinger.com
How to Fix a Credit Report Error
www.kiplinger.com/basics/archives/2002/05/story15.html

Disability Insurance

About Disability Insurance
www.about-disability-insurance.com

Divorce

DivorceNet
www.divorcenet.com

Divorce Support
www.divorcesupport.com

Fisher, B. 2005. *Rebuilding: When Your Relationship Ends* (3rd ed.). Atascadero, CA: Impact Publishers, Inc.

Ricci, I. 1997. *Mom's House, Dad's House: Making Two Homes for Your Child*. New York: Fireside

Estate Taxes

Internal Revenue Service
Frequently Asked Questions on Estate Taxes
www.irs.gov/businesses/small/article/0,,id=108143,00.html

Fair Debt Collection Practices Act

U.S. Federal Trade Commission
www.ftc.gov/bcp/edu/pubs/consumer/credit/cre18.shtm

Financial Risk Quiz

MoneyCentral at MSN.com
http://moneycentral.msn.com/investor/calcs/n_riskq/main.asp

529 Plans

Saving for College
www.savingforcollege.com

Gambling

Gamblers Anonymous
www.gamblersanonymous.org

National Council on Problem Gambling
1-800-522-4700
www.ncpgambling.org

Gift Tax

Internal Revenue Service
Frequently Asked Questions on Gift Tax
www.irs.gov/businesses/small/article/0,,id=108139,00.html

Governmental Aid for Children Under Five Years Old

Special Supplemental Nutrition Program for Women, Infants, and
Children (WIC Program)
United States Department of Agriculture, Food and Nutrition Service
(Telephone numbers vary by state.)
www.fns.usda.gov/wic

Health Care Surrogate Forms

Caring Connections
www.caringinfo.org/stateaddownload

Hospice
www.hospicenet.org/html/directives.html

U.S. Living Will Registry
www.uslivingwillregistry.com/forms.shtm

Health Insurance

CNNMoney.com
Money101. Lesson 16: Health Insurance
http://money.cnn.com/magazines/moneymag/money101/lesson16/

eHealthInsurance
1-800-977-8860
www.ehealthinsurance.com

Health Insurance for Children

U.S. Department of Health and Human Services
Insure Kids Now!: Linking the Nation's Children to Health Insurance
1-877-KIDS-NOW (1-877-543-7669)
www.insurekidsnow.gov

Insurance Claims Clearinghouse

Medical Information Bureau
1-866-692-6901 (for MIB record information)
www.mib.com

Investment Research

CNNMoney.com
http://money.cnn.com

Google Finance
www.google.com/finance

Yahoo Finance
www.finance.yahoo.com

Labeling Machines

Brother
www.brother.com

DYMO
www.dymo.com

Laptop Security Locks

Computer Security Products, Inc.
www.computersecurity.com

Kensington Computer Products Group
www.kensington.com

Lemon Laws

Lemon Law America
www.lemonlawamerica.com

Life Insurance

Smart Money
How Much Life Insurance Do You Need?
www.smartmoney.com/personal-finance/insurance/how-much-life
-insurance-do-you-need-12949/

Smart Money
Term or Whole Life?
www.smartmoney.com/insurance/life/index.cfm?story=lifeterm

Loan Forgiveness

AmeriCorps
www.americorps.gov

Federal Student Aid
Cancellation/Deferment Options for Teachers
http://studentaid.ed.gov/PORTALSWebApp/students/english/teachercancel.
jsp?tab=repaying

Federal Student Aid
Loan Forgiveness for Public Service Employees
http://studentaid.ed.gov/students/attachments/siteresources/
LoanForgivenessv4.pdf

FinAid
Loan Forgiveness
www.finaid.org/loans/forgiveness.phtml

Loan Information

Center for Responsible Lending
www.responsiblelending.org

Marriage and Family Therapists

The Family and Marriage Counseling Directory
www.family-marriage-counseling.com

The American Association for Marriage and Family Therapy
Therapist Locator Directory
www.therapistlocator.net

Money Management Software

Microsoft Money
www.microsoft.com/money

Quicken
www.quicken.intuit.com

Mortgage Refinancing

CNNMoney.com
Mortgage Refinancing Calculator
http://cgi.money.cnn.com/tools/cutmortgage/cutmortgage.html

Mutual Funds

SmartMoney.com
www.smartmoney.com/licensing/funds/fundfeeanalyzer.html

Negotiating

Fisher, R., and D. Ertel. 1995. *Getting Ready to Negotiate: The Getting to Yes Workbook*. New York: Penguin Books

Fisher, R., B. Patton, and W. Ury. 1992. *Getting to Yes: Negotiating Agreement without Giving In*. 2nd ed. New York: Penguin Books

Office Supply Stores

Office Depot
1-800-GODEPOT (1-800-403-3768)
www.officedepot.com

Office Max
1-800-283-7674
www.officemax.com

Staples
1-800-378-2753
www.staples.com

Online Backups

Amazon Simple Storage Service (S3)
http://aws.amazon.com/s3/

Mozy
http://mozy.com

Organizational Products

The Container Store
www.containerstore.com

Stacks and Stacks
www.stacksandstacks.com

Target
www.target.com

Password and PIN Storage

KeePass
www.keepass.info

Password Safe
http://passwordsafe.sourceforge.net

Payday Loan Caution

Federal Trade Commission
"FTC Consumer Alert: Payday Loans Equal Very Costly Cash:
Consumers Urged to Consider the Alternatives"
1-877-FTC-HELP (1-877-382-4357)
www.ftc.gov/bcp/edu/pubs/consumer/alerts/alt060.shtm

Personal Finance

Dave Ramsey
www.daveramsey.com

Morris, K. M., and V. B. Morris. 2000. *The Wall Street Journal Guide to Personal Finance*. New York: Lightbulb Press, Inc.

Orman, S. 1997. *The Nine Steps to Financial Freedom: Practical and Spiritual Steps So You Can Stop Worrying*. New York: Crown Publishers

Orman, S. 2008. *The Road to Wealth: The Answers You Need to More Than 2,000 Personal Finance Questions*. New York: Riverhead Books

Tyson, E. 2006. *Personal Finance for Dummies* (5th ed.). Hoboken, NJ: Wiley Publishing Inc.

Receipt Scanner

NeatReceipts Scanner
1-866-632-8732
www.neatco.com

Recipe Lookup

All Recipes
www.allrecipes.com

Epicurious
www.epicurious.com

Retirement Calculator

CNNMoney.com
http://cgi.money.cnn.com/tools/retirementplanner/retirementplanner.jsp

MSN Money
http://moneycentral.msn.com/retire/planner.aspx

Social Security

U.S. Social Security Administration
www.ssa.gov

U.S. Social Security Administration
Social Security calculator
www.ssa.gov/planners/calculators.htm

Special Needs Trusts

Elias, S. R. 2007. *Special Needs Trusts: Providing for Your Child's Financial Future.* Berkeley, CA: Nolo

Student Loans

Federal Student Aid Information Center
1-800-4-FED-AID (1-800-433-3243)
www.studentaid.ed.gov

Financial Aid Information Page
www.finaid.org

Free Application for Student Aid (FAFSA)
1-800-4-FED-AID (1-800-433-3243)
www.fafsa.ed.gov

HEATH Resource Center
George Washington University
1-202-973-0904
www.heath.gwu.edu

Tax Software

H&R Block
www.hrblock.com/taxes/products/software/index.html

TurboTax
www.turbotax.intuit.com

Travel Tips and Suggestions

My Travel Guide
www.mytravelguide.com

Trip Advisor
www.tripadvisor.com

Zagat
www.zagat.com

Travel Tips and Suggestions

Rick Steves Europe
www.ricksteves.com

U.S. Currency

Bureau of Engraving and Printing
US Department of the Treasury
Washington, DC, Tour: 1-866-874-2330 or 1-202-874-2330
Fort Worth, Texas, Tour: 1-866-865-1194 or 1-817-231-4000
www.moneyfactory.gov

U.S. Mint
U.S. Department of the Treasury
Denver, Colorado, Tour: 1-303-405-4761
Philadelphia, Pennsylvania, Tour: 1-215-408-0110
www.usmint.gov

References

American Bankruptcy Institute. 2009. March Consumer Bankruptcy Filings Increase 41 Percent Over Last Year. Press release. April 2. Alexandria, VA: Author. Retrieved April 21, 2009, from www.abiworld.org/AM /Template.cfm?Section=Home&TEMPLATE=/CM/ContentDisplay. cfm&CONTENTID=57080.

American Psychiatric Association. 2004. *Diagnostic and Statistical Manual of Mental Disorders*, 4th ed. rev. Washington, DC: Author.

Barkley, R. A. 2005. *Attention-Deficit Hyperactivity Disorder: A Handbook for Diagnosis and Treatment*, 3rd ed. New York: The Guilford Press.

Barkley, R. A., K. R. Murphy, and M. Fischer. 2008. *ADHD in Adults: What the Science Says*. New York: The Guilford Press.

Bernard, T. S. 2008. The key to wedded bliss? Money matters. *The New York Times* (September 10), SPG5.

Biederman, J., C. Petty, R. Fried, J. Fontanella, A. E. Doyle, L. J. Seidman, and S. V. Faraone. 2006. Impact of psychometrically defined deficits of executive functioning in adults with attention deficit hyperactivity disorder. *American Journal of Psychiatry* 163(10):1730–38.

Biederman, J., M. C. Monuteaux, T. Spencer, T. E. Wilens, H. A. MacPherson, and S. V. Faraone. 2008. Stimulant therapy and risk for subsequent substance use disorders in male adults with ADHD: A naturalistic controlled 10-year follow-up study. *American Journal of Psychiatry* 165(5): 597–603.

Biederman, J., S. V. Faraone, T. J. Spencer, E. Mick, M. C. Monuteaux, and M. Aleardi. 2006. Functional impairment in adults with self-reports of diagnosed ADHD: A controlled study of 1001 adults in the community. *Journal of Clinical Psychiatry* 67: 524–40.

Biederman, J., S. W. Ball, M. C. Monuteaux, E. Mick, T. J. Spencer, M. McCreary, M. Cote, and S. V. Faraone. 2008. New insights into the comorbidity between ADHD and major depression in adolescent and young adult females. *Journal of the American Academy of Child and Adolescent Psychiatry* 47(4):426–34.

Bowen, R., D. Chavira, K. Bailey, M. Stein, and M. Stein. 2007. Nature of anxiety comorbid with attention deficit hyperactivity disorder in children from a pediatric primary care setting. *Psychiatry Research* 157(1):201–9.

Brunsvold, G. L., G. Oepen, E. J. Federman, and R. Akins. 2008. Comorbid depression and ADHD in children and adolescents. *Psychiatric Times* 25(10; September 1).

Clifford, C. 2008. Personal income in largest drop in 3 years (August 29). Retrieved January 31, 2009, from http://money.cnn.com/2008/08/29/news/economy/consumer_spending/index.htm?postversion=2008082911.

College Board. 2008. *Trends in College Pricing.* Trends in Higher Education Series. Washington, DC: Author.

Consumer Federation of America. 2008. Overdraft loan fees increase at nation's ten largest banks: Federal Reserve proposal fails to protect consumers from unauthorized loans. Press release (August 6). Washington DC: Author. From www.consumerfed.org/pdfs/Overdraft_Comments_press_release_8-6-08.pdf.

Dreschler, R., P. Rizzo, and H. C. Steinhausen. 2008. Decision-making on an explicit risk-taking task in preadolescents with attention-deficit/hyperactivity disorder. *Journal of Neural Transmission* 15(2):201–9.

Eakin, L., K. Minde, L. Hechtman, E. Ochs, E. Krane, R. Bouffard, B. Greenfield, and K. Looper. 2004. The marital and family functioning of adults with ADHD and their spouses. *Journal of Attention Disorders* 8(1):1–10.

Federal Deposit Insurance Corporation (FDIC). 2008. FDIC Study of Bank Overdraft Programs. Report (November). Washington, DC: Author. From www.fdic.gov/bank/analytical/overdraft/FDIC138_ExecutiveSummary_v508.pdf.

Grant, K. B. 2007. Five sneaky bank fees (April 13). Retrieved January 31, 2009, from www.smartmoney.com/spending/deals/five-sneaky-bank-fees-21096/.

Kessler, R. C., L. Adler, R. Barkley, J. Biederman, C. K. Conners, O. Demler, S. V. Faraone, et al. 2006. The prevalence and correlates of adult ADHD in the United States: Results from the National Comorbidity Survey Replication. *American Journal of Psychiatry* 163(4):716–23.

Kirk, B., and E. Young. 2007. Cash windfall can lead to downfall. *The Eagle-Tribune* (October 28).

Knouse, L. E., C. L. Bagwell, R. A. Barkley, and K. R. Murphy. 2005. Accuracy of self-evaluation in adults with ADHD: Evidence from a driving study. *Journal of Attention Disorders* 8(4):221–34.

Koba, M. 2009. Paying for college: 529 plans won't cover the cost anymore (April 16). Retrieved May 11, 2009 from www.cnbc.com/id/29897315.

Lovell, P., and J. Isaacs. 2008. *The Impact of the Mortgage Crisis on Children.* Washington, DC: First Focus.

Mannuzza, S., R. G. Klein, N. L. Truong, J. L. Moulton, E. R. Roizen, K. H. Howell, and F. X. Castellanos. 2008. Age of methylphenidate treatment initiation in children with ADHD and later substance abuse: Prospective follow-up into adulthood. *American Journal of Psychiatry* 165(5):604–9.

Matza, L. S., C. Paramore, and M. Prasad. 2005. A review of the economic burden of ADHD. *Cost Effectiveness and Resource Allocation* 3(June 9):5.

Minde, K., L. Eakin, L. Hechtman, E. Ochs, R. Bouffard, B. Greenfield, and K. Looper. 2003. The psychosocial functioning of children and spouses of adults with ADHD. *Journal of Child Psychology and Psychiatry* 44(4):637–46.

Pietras, C. J., D. R. Cherek, S. D. Lane, O. V. Tcheremissine, and J. L. Steinberg. 2003. Effects of methylphenidate on impulsive choice in adult humans. *Psychopharmacology* 170(4):390–98.

Prelec, D., and D. Simester. 2001. Always leave home without it: A further investigation of the credit-card effect on willingness to pay. *Marketing Letters* 12(1):5–12.

Realtytrac. 2007. *Year-End 2007 Metropolitan Foreclosure Market Report.* Irvine, CA: Author.

Rietveld, M. J. H., J. J. Hudziak, M. Bartels, C. E. M. Beijsterveldt, and D. I. Boomsma. 2004. Heritability of attention problems in children: Longitudinal results from a study of twins, age 3 to 12. *Journal of Child Psychology and Psychiatry* 45(3):577–88.

Rodriguez-Jimenez, R., C. Avila, M. A. Jimenez-Arriero, G. Ponce, R. Monasor, M. Jimenez, M. Aragües, J. Hoenicka, G. Rubio, and T. Palomo. 2006. Impulsivity and sustained attention in pathological gamblers: Influence of childhood ADHD history. *Journal of Gambling Studies* 22(4):451–61.

Rooney, B. 2008. Bankruptcy filings surge to 1 million—up 29%. *CNN Money* (October 27). http://money.cnn.com/2008/08/27/news/economy/bankruptcy/index.htm.

Sarkis, S. 2004. Therapy and insurance (letter to the editor). *Smart Money* 13(7):10.

Secnik, K., A. Swensen, and M. J. Lage. 2005. Comorbidities and costs of adult patients diagnosed with attention-deficit hyperactivity disorder. *Pharmacoeconomics* 23(1):93–102.

Smart Money. 2008. They'll never know: Eight hidden ways to cut wedding costs (June 11). Retrieved October 26, 2008, from www.smartmoney.com/personal-finance/marriage-divorce/theyll-never-know-eight-hidden-ways-to-cut-wedding-costs-13918/.

Soat, J. 2007. Thoughts on dealing with identity theft. *InformationWeek*, 1, 129(March 12):60.

Swensen, A., H. G. Birnbaum, R. B. Hamadi, P. Greenberg, P. Y. Cremieux, and Secnik, K. 2004. Incidence and costs of accidents among attention-deficit/hyperactivity disorder patients. *Journal of Adolescent Health* 35(4):346–7.

U.S. Department of Agriculture, Center for Nutrition Policy and Promotion. 2007. *Expenditures on Children by Families, 2007* (Misc. Publication Number 1528–2007).

U.S. Department of Education, National Center for Education Statistics. 2004. Debt burden of college graduates. Retrieved February 4, 2009, from http://nces.ed.gov/programs/coe/2004/section5/indicator38.asp.

Wilens, T. E. 2004. Attention-deficit/hyperactivity disorder and the substance use disorders: The nature of the relationship, subtypes at risk, and treatment issues. *Psychiatric Clinics of North America* 27(2):283–301.

Wolf, J. R., H. R. Arkes, and W. A. Muhanna. 2008. The power of touch: An examination of the effect of duration of physical contact on the valuation of objects. *Judgment and Decision Making* 3(6):476–82.

Worthy, S. L., L. Blinn-Pike, and J. Jonkman. 2008. Having mom and dad pay for college: Financial advantage or disadvantage? *Consumer Interests Annual* 54: 185–88.

Stephanie Moulton Sarkis, Ph.D., is adjunct assistant professor at Florida Atlantic University in Boca Raton, FL, and author of *10 Simple Solutions to Adult ADD* and *Making the Grade with ADD*. She is a nationally certified counselor and a licensed mental health counselor, and has a private counseling practice where she specializes in ADD/ADHD counseling and coaching. Sarkis won an American Psychological Association Outstanding Dissertation Award in 2001, and has been published in the *Journal of Attention Disorders*. She has made media appearances on CNN's *Health Minute, Fox News, ABC News, Sirius Satellite Radio, First Business Television,* and numerous other networks and stations. She was also featured in the book *The Gift of Adult ADD*. Visit her online at www.stephaniesarkis.com.

Karl Klein, JD, is a licensed attorney in the state of Florida. He graduated from the University of Florida College of Law with high honors and holds degrees in finance and insurance. A former associate with White & Case, LLP, one of the world's largest law firms, he currently has a private practice in Miami, FL.

Foreword writer **Harvey C. Parker, Ph.D.,** is cofounder of Children and Adults with Attention-Deficit/Hyperactivity Disorder (CHADD).

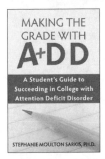
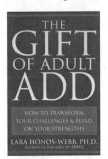